WALKING GRATEFULLY

A Camino Story

RICHARD RAY

RESOURCE *Publications* · Eugene, Oregon

WALKING GRATEFULLY

This memoir is dedicated to Craig Kleinheksel, a friend for whom I am very grateful. St. Augustine explains friendship better than I can: *. . . if poverty pinches, if grief saddens, if bodily pain disturbs, if exile discourages, if any other disaster torments, provided there are present human beings who not only know how to rejoice with those in joy, but also to weep with those who weep (Romans 12:15) and can speak and converse in a helpful way, those rough spots are smoothed, the heavy burdens are lightened, and adversity is overcome.*[1]

1. Hill and Rotelle, *Letters*, 185.

And when you turn to the right or when you turn to the left,
your ears shall hear a word behind you, saying,
"This is the way; walk in it."

—Isa 30:21

Contents

Introduction

CRAIG and I left the Valcarlos *albergue* at 6:30. It was a cold May morning. The freezing drizzle did not take long to find its way through our rain jackets. The town was preternaturally quiet. There were no other pilgrims about. We walked along the paved road for a couple of miles with no fear of passing vehicles. They were still asleep too. The *flechas amarillas* (yellow arrows) eventually guided us onto the leaf-litter path in the dark, dripping woods. Within five minutes our lower bodies and feet were as sodden as our shoulders and arms. The higher we climbed, the colder the rain became. Craig eventually lost all feeling in both of his drizzle-exposed hands. I gave him my gloves and that helped a bit, but he still suffered. I knew my left knee would have problems with this climb, but I did not anticipate the messages my right knee was also sending me. The ascent was very tough—especially the last two hours through the near-vertical section just before the Ibañeta Pass. We rested every five minutes to reset the triphammers that were our beating hearts. Honestly, we could not tell if we were soaked by the freezing rain or the perspiration occasioned by the exertion of the climb. We eventually reached the top in a drizzly fog with scattered springtime snowflakes littering the ground—snowflakes that bore some resemblance to those of Longfellow's imagination:

Out of the bosom of the Air,
    Out of the cloud-folds of her garments shaken,
    Over the woodlands brown and bare,
    Over the harvest-fields forsaken,
        Silent, and soft, and slow
        Descends the snow.

Even as our cloudy fancies take
    Suddenly shape in some divine expression,

Even as the troubled heart doth make
    In the white countenance confession,
        The troubled sky reveals
        The grief it feels.

This is the poem of the air,
    Slowly in silent syllables recorded;

This is the secret of despair,
    Long in its cloudy bosom hoarded,
        Now whispered and revealed
        To wood and field.[1]

Chilled and tired, we began the gradual, twenty-minute descent to Roncesvalles. The Pyrenees were behind us.

**The climb over the Pyrenees was cold, damp, and steep.
(Photo by Marc Noorman on Unsplash)**

1. Longfellow, "Snow-flakes."

Preparing Mind, Body, and Spirit

Put my life in order, O my God.[2]

Be careful about where you send your children to school. They will make friends there. You will eventually befriend their schoolmates' parents. Your new friends will become an important part of your social circle for decades to come. Such was the case for us. Carol and I walked our eldest child to the front door of Longfellow School, his little hand tightly gripping Carol's as we turned him over to Mrs. Larkin's gentle and loving instruction. Craig and Dar did the same with their first child. And so began a friendship that would last until the present day. Carol and Dar would join the same weekly sewing circle—something known to all as the "S & B Ladies." These days there is more good-natured bitching than stitching accomplished at their weekly, Wednesday night conclaves. Craig and I would see each other at school and neighborhood gatherings. From time to time when the ladies got together we banished husbands retreated to someone's porch for a beer or two and tales that grew taller with each empty bottle. Thirty-five years after that fateful day at Longfellow School—our children now grown with children of their own—Craig invited me out to lunch and wanted to learn more about my 2016 pilgrimage to Santiago de Compostela.[3] After a few such lunches—and some artfully conducted diplomacy with Carol and Dar—we made plans to walk the Camino together in May–June 2019.

Be careful where you send your children to school.

Planning began in earnest around September 2018. We began walking as a way to prepare our feet, legs, and lungs for the exertions that awaited us in France and Spain. We usually walked alone, but once or twice every week we met downtown and went for a six-miler while we talked about every subject in the encyclopedia. My left knee began giving me serious problems. Things eventually progressed to the point where I needed a cane just to walk around the apartment. Surgery in December revealed Stage 3 osteoarthritis and two torn menisci. The doctor clipped out the damaged portions of the cartilage and told me I could exercise as my pain allowed. Would I be able to walk the Camino as I desired? Time would tell.

2. Unless otherwise noted, all epigrams/epigraphs are from Aquinas, *Aquinas Prayer Book*.

3. Ray, *The Shape of My Heart*.

3

Winter in Holland, Michigan is snowy, cold, and long. Craig and I walked through some very challenging weather in an effort to coax our sixtysomething bodies into shape for our adventure. While my knee injury would not permit me to run, climb stairs, and trudge up sand dunes as I did in preparation for the 2016 pilgrimage, I was determined to make sure that I walked at least 500 miles before leaving for the 2019 stroll of the same distance. It was often hard to rise from a warm bed and step into the icy darkness for this purpose. But I did it—and so did Craig.

Springtime pilgrimages require long wintertime walks.

During our long period of training Carol frequently asked me why I wanted to return to the Camino. Hadn't the 2016 pilgrimage helped me resolve the anger and the vocational bewilderment from which I so desperately desired relief during that season of grief? My spirit prior to the first pilgrimage was much like that of Lewis's allegorical Vertue in *Pilgrim's Regress*:[4]

> John [Vertue's traveling companion], I do not know what is coming over me. Long ago you asked me . . . where I was going and why: and I remember that I brushed the question aside. At that time it seemed to me so much more important to keep my rules and do my thirty miles a day. But I am beginning to find that it

4. Lewis, *Pilgrim's Regress*, 121.

will not do. In the old days it was always a question of doing what I chose instead of what I wanted: but now I am beginning to be uncertain what it is I choose.

The 2016 pilgrimage helped cure me of this *ennui*. But this was by no means a forgone conclusion. Why couldn't I simply adopt an attitude of the Stoic philosopher, Epictetus?

Some things are up to us and some are not up to us.[5]

Oh, how I wish it was so simple as that. I knew—on an intellectual level— that God *could* heal me, but *would* he? And what would healing look like? Would it assume the form I desired, that I wanted, that I planned? Or would it involve the cross, and death to self? Like Thomas Merton before he accepted his vocation,[6] I was dilly-dallying about trying to *think* my way back to happiness.

The 2016 pilgrimage had such a profound impact on my spirit that I wanted to go back to the Camino as a kind of longform devotion of gratitude. I resolved that the stone representing my anger that I carried in 2016 to Cruz de Ferro[7] would be replaced by the stones representing the burdens of others in 2019. I contacted approximately thirty friends, told them of my plans, explained the Cruz de Ferro tradition, and offered to carry their stones to the foot of the cross in that high, lonesome place. As I trudged through the long winter of preparation my sense of gratitude welled up within me, filling my days and nights.

Craig and I also prepared mentally for the pilgrimage. We are both planners by nature and preference, so we did what planners do: we planned. Some pilgrims eschew planning, considering schemes of this sort to be the feverish anxieties of Type A control freaks determined to strip the Camino

---

5. Epictetus, *Handbook*, 11.

6. Merton, *Seven Storey Mountain*, 265.

7. Cruz de Ferro occupies nearly the highest point of the entire Camino Francés (there's a slightly higher pass after Manjarín). The site consists of a tall wooden pole topped with an iron cross. This is said to be an ancient monument, first erected by the ancient Celts, then dedicated by the Romans to their god Mercury (protector of travelers), and later crowned by the cross and renamed as a Christian site by the ninth-century hermit Gaucelmo. For centuries, pilgrims have brought a stone to the place (either from home or the flatlands below) to represent their burden. The stone and the burden are left here, leaving the pilgrim lighter (literally and figuratively) for the journey ahead. Today all sorts of symbolic items are left behind, and some stones bear written messages (Gitlitz and Davidson, *Pilgrimage Road to Santiago*, 284).

of any possible mystery, spontaneity, or serendipity. Well, this seems overly judgmental. We made a rough outline of where we thought we would walk each day. We planned our transport to and from Saint-Jean-Pied-de-Port and Santiago de Compostela. We outlined our transport and accommodation for the ten-day vacation we would enjoy with Carol and Dar when they met us at the conclusion of our pilgrimage. And we also took a page out of the 2016 pilgrimage that Joe and I walked by honestly and transparently discussing our concerns. I was worried about my knee. Craig was worried about being sixty-five years old and walking 500 miles. Would his small, family-run business thrive in his absence? Would we become heartsore from the absence of loved ones? Would homesickness cripple us? Talking about these concerns helped us develop a calmer spirit than we might have otherwise carried with us along The Way.

On The Road. Finally.

O merciful God, grant that I may desire ardently, search prudently, recognize truly, and bring to perfect completion whatever is pleasing to You for the praise and glory of Your Name.

— AQUINAS, *AQUINAS PRAYER BOOK*

Craig and I were scheduled to leave for Spain on April 30. Fortunately, I was able to read and mark all my students' papers, submit final grades, and generally wrap up the semester just in time. As our departure approached it seemed as if I could hear each tick of the clock. April 29 was taken up with attending to last-minute items on my to-do list—returning library books, meeting a friend for coffee, picking up the last stone from Bill Moreau, a stone that was prayed over by his entire Senior Seminar class. It was a meaningful rock. But mostly the day was about sitting around waiting to leave and double-checking my backpack to make sure I'd packed everything.

Chapter 1

Grand Rapids to Saint-Jean-Pied-de-Port

Grant that I may know what You require me to do.

— *Aquinas, Aquinas Prayer Book*

O UR flight from Grand Rapids, Michigan was badly delayed due to inclement weather elsewhere. Were it not for the ticketing agent's diligence and good humor we would have missed our Barcelona connection and been delayed by a day. But she rerouted us through different cities, both in the US and Europe, and we arrived in Barcelona with time to spare before our short hop to San Sebastián. God bless you, Airport Lady.

Various airport security agents took exception to certain elements of my baggage. The TSA agent in Grand Rapids was not crazy about the thirty stones I was carrying.

"Why are you traveling with a bag of rocks?" he inquired politely but with a tone of officious authority. When I told him what they were for, and what they represented, he looked at me like I had something stuck between my teeth and replied "Ooooookay then" as he allowed me to pass.

The security agent in Barcelona was concerned about my small, backpack-sized umbrella, apparently concerned that it could be used for sinister purposes. He also saw something on the x-ray that he did not like. After running his practiced hands expertly over the outside of my pack he grunted a phrase in Catalan that communicated his confidence that I posed no threat.

Julien, the van driver from Express Bourricot, met us at the San Sebastián airport for the ninety-minute drive to Saint-Jean-Pied-de-Port. We shared the ride with four Swedes who had a couple of weeks of holiday and planned to walk part of the Camino. Julien was a young man with a master's degree in environmental science who couldn't find a job in or around St. Jean, so he drove a van shuttling pilgrims to their destinations. He was a pleasant conversation partner as the van meandered through mountain valleys surrounded by forested slopes reaching up to a leaden sky that promised rain.

Julien dropped us off near the Pilgrim Office, where we obtained our first *sello*—the stamp placed into our pilgrim *credencial* that would eventually be joined by the *sellos* of each place we stopped along the Camino. Once we were "official" we strolled down the Rue de la Citadelle in search of our *albergue*. Craig spotted a sporting goods store along the way and purchased a pair of hiking poles. They were less expensive than I imagined. Had I known this, I would have left my poles at home and simply purchased some in France as Craig did. I ended up paying more to transport my poles from home than I would have had to spend to buy them locally and donate them to a pilgrim in need at the end of the Camino. Oh well.

Eric the *hospitalero* greeted us warmly when we arrived at Le Chemin vers l'Etoile—our home for the evening. He took his time checking us into his 500-year-old *gite*. He explained that he used to live in the Paris rat-race, but finally chucked it all for the life he now enjoyed in this quaint, charming village.

"I now have no money, but I LOVE what I do," he gushed as he escorted us to the third floor and our shared bunkroom.

Though we were wrung out from the many hours of travel, it was early for bed, so we walked down the street in search of dinner. We were both mannequin-quiet, and spent most of the meal lost in our own pensive thoughts. I suppose the combination of sleep deprivation, eagerness to begin the pilgrimage, and first-day jitters combined to dull our normally easy conversation. When we returned to the *gite* to get ready for bed one of the pilgrims sharing our bunkroom told us that the Pilgrim Office registered 600 people who started The Way earlier in the day.[1] This was causing overcrowding problems at Roncesvalles, Zubiri, and Larrasoaña—with people resorting to taxis to shepherd them as far away as Pamplona to find beds. This intelligence weighed heavy on my mind as I slipped into my bunk and eventually drifted off to sleep, grateful for a safe arrival.

1. The Camino has become wildly popular since being reestablished in the 1980s and popularized by Emilio Estevez's film *The Way* in 2010. Nearly 350,000 pilgrims from nearly every nation received their *compostela* in 2019 (Oficina de Acogida al Perigrino, Catedral de Santiago, *Informe Estadístico*, 1).

Chapter 2

Saint-Jean-Pied-de-Port to Valcarlos

Bestow upon me the power to accomplish Your will,
as is necessary and fitting for the salvation of my soul.
— Aquinas, Aquinas Prayer Book

J ET lag is a problem for me when I travel abroad. I typically require an adjustment period of one day for every hour of time difference to sleep through the night. Would I have to wait a week to equilibrate on this trip? Time would tell, but Night One was rough. I fell asleep easily, but by 2:00 a.m. I was wide awake and ready to rock. When Craig awoke around 6:00 he told me that he experienced a tense moment in the middle of the night. A fellow pilgrim poked him awake and accused him—in a language Craig did not understand—of stealing his bunk, which almost turned into a heated moment. Craig stood his ground though, once again proving that possession is 90 percent of the law the world over.

Though our morning routine would eventually resemble a well-choreographed dance in the dark, we stumbled around like drunken sailors on shore-leave during our first morning. We would eventually learn how to put our few possessions in the same place without fail or deviation of any kind before going to bed each night. Once this habit was well ingrained, we would simply open our eyes upon awakening, plant our feet on the floor, gather our things without needing to see them, and carry our gear quietly out of the bunkroom and into the hallway or a common room to avoid disturbing our slumbering brethren. But not that morning. We dropped things. We rustled our bags. We turned on our headlamps. When we finally cleared out of the bunkroom, we realized that we had forgotten things and had to go back in, admitting light and making additional noise. We were crummy pilgrims on Morning Number One. If you were there and you are reading this, forgive us. We feel bad about it.

After a wee nibble and a quick gulp of lukewarm coffee in the *gite's* kitchen we stepped into the main street and pointed our determined faces westward just as the sky began to brighten. Ten minutes later we passed the village limits and headed toward Valcarlos, our destination for the day. Unlike the Napoleon Route that heads directly up to the high country, the Valcarlos Route follows the course of the Nive d'Arnéguy/Rio Luzaide through a lovely forested valley with relatively mild grades. Our walk on Day Two—which would take us from Valcarlos to Roncesvalles and on to Espinal—would test our stamina with its steep slopes and rapid elevation changes. While most pilgrims choose the high route for its long views and its *Sound of Music* ambiance, we decided to take our time and warm up our legs by dividing the typical first day's distance into two sections with gentler elevation gains on the initial walk.[1] With age comes wisdom, or so we hoped.

Our first day of pilgriming only required twelve kilometers of walking—all through bucolic landscapes. The way was well marked, and ran over narrow farm roads with barely any traffic. We saw no other pilgrims, and wondered if the rumor we heard the night before about the Great Pilgrim Horde was unfounded or perhaps exaggerated. In any case, it felt wonderful to exercise our legs after spending so much time in airplanes and vans over the past forty-eight hours.

A couple of hours after we left St. Jean we stumbled into the village of Arnéguy. It was right next to the main highway that runs through the valley connecting France with Pamplona and points west. There was a cafe

---

1. The route from what is now France to what is now Spain was trod by the Romans as they made their way to gold mines in the Astorga region. They preferred the higher, more exposed path—now called the Napoleon Route—because the lower route through the valley near Valcarlos was famous for its bandits lurking in the forest, ready to take advantage of unprepared passersby (Gitlitz and Davidson, *Pilgrimage Road to Santiago*, 55).

there where we enjoyed our first of what would be many, many *cafe con leches*. Pilgrims everywhere assume a dreamy countenance as they wax poetic about this beverage. A potent jolt of espresso is blended with warm, frothed milk until it takes on the color of melted caramel. When a sugar packet is emptied onto the foamy surface the glistening crystal granules sit momentarily, as if resting upon a cloud ascending to heaven, before gradually giving way to gravity and melting into the creamy depths. Paradise in a cup.

There are no pilgriming problems that can't be solved with this.
(Photo by Jon Tyson on Unsplash)

We crossed the river—and by doing so left France behind—and climbed the steep hill that led to the village where we would spend our first night in Spain: Valcarlos. Joe and I stumbled around looking for the *albergue* when we stayed here in 2016. Now that I knew my way around, Craig and I were able to walk directly to the small grocery store/bar/restaurant/hardware store/five-and-dime/wine shop and confidently request the code to the *albergue* door—located across the street in the lower level of the village primary school. Yes, in that place they allow transient hobos to sleep in the same building where small children gather. We did our best to improve the general image of transient hobos.

France on the left, Spain on the right.

Our short first day resulted in an early arrival. We had the entire afternoon to explore Valcarlos's many charms. But before our cultural immersion in this valley of delights could begin . . . *lunch*. The *tienda* had a good stock of comestibles. Spanish chorizo and Basque cheese on fresh baguettes made for a tasty mid-day meal. Lunch being one of my three favorite meals of the day, I was reminded of the virtues of that underappreciated source of daily happiness—the sandwich.

After a shower, laundry, and a nap we walked around the village, visited the cemetery, and explored the small museum dedicated to the Basque culture and history of the Valcarlos area. I should note here that we visited many cemeteries as our journey continued. As a third-generation funeral director, Craig's interest in all things funereal is seemingly boundless—and understandably so. On a Valcarlos hillside, with stunning views of the Pyrenean highlands all around us, Craig gloried in his first Iberian burial ground. It was a moment of particular poignancy.

Craig surveys the final resting place of the citizens of Valcarlos.

Just as we were beginning to think that the Camino had been emptied of pilgrims, Danny from Merida, Spain joined us in the Valcarlos *albergue*. He started from St. Jean on the same morning as we did, but found the walking difficult, thus arriving long after we settled in. He spoke no English, so I served as the official interpreter when he and Craig wanted to talk. We had a delightful time stumbling past language barriers by showing each other photos of our families and hometowns while sharing a supper of a large salad with all the trimmings the local shop could provide. To our great dismay, Danny snored like a freight train racing a fighter jet. He was a very pleasant fellow though. I worried about whether his lack of physical fitness would allow him to walk the Camino as he desired, for he was a portly gentleman. We never saw him again.

I was grateful for a good first day of walking. God's many blessings seemed abundant indeed as the sky dimmed and I nestled in for what I hoped would be a good night of sleep in that mountain hamlet.

Chapter 3

Valcarlos to Espinal

Grant to me, O Lord my God, that I may not falter in times of prosperity or adversity, so that I may not be exalted in the former, nor dejected in the latter.
— *Aquinas, Aquinas Prayer Book*

I F you have read this far you know that our walk from Valcarlos to Espinal was a cold, wet, steep, hard, slippery, numbing trudge. When Joe and I walked this route in 2016 we found it to be a pleasant, leafy amble through forested glades. Yes, it was steep, but in an athletically satisfying way that satiated one's desires for healthful, manly exercise.

A physical challenge worthy of virtuous pursuit.

But 2019 was not 2016. The climb with Craig reminded me that prayer is good, and dying with a prayer on one's lips is even better. So I prayed just in case my heart decided to abandon its natural purpose. It did not. Another thing for which I could be grateful.

Craig and I discussed the pilgrim overcrowding problem during our walk from St. Jean to Valcarlos. We eventually decided on a three-part strategy. First, we would do our best to stay in nonstage towns. The guidebooks often carried by pilgrims typically divide the route into stages of lengths which the average pilgrim should be able to walk in one day's time. Consequently, many pilgrims compete with each other for a bed in the *albergues* in those stage towns. We reasoned that seeking accommodation in nonstage towns should help us avoid the crowds. We would also try to make reservations a couple of days in advance of where we thought we would seek shelter for the night. As I explained earlier, many pilgrims consider this to be a sin against the spirit of the Camino. My thinking was that we could either avoid reservations and walk with the anxiety of not finding a bed, or we could make reservations and enjoy the day, confident that we had a place to lay our heads at night. Purists be damned. Our final strategy would be to rise early from our beds in an effort to begin and end each day's walk before most other pilgrims. Gentlemen of a certain age don't/can't sleep in anyway, so this wasn't much of a sacrifice to the spirit of the Camino but more of a nod to urological realities.

We walked past Roncesvalles without stopping for a look-around, lest we freeze solid. We had originally planned to stay there, but Roncesvalles is the mothership of stage towns for the early part of the Camino. We needed to put some miles between it and its huddled, lesser denizens enslaved to their guidebooks. Espinal was only another few miles up the path.

We had enjoyed no refreshment so far on that gray, sodden day. Hungry and thirsty, we stumbled to a cafe in the next town after Roncesvalles—Burguete—for *cafe con leche* and *tortilla patata*. Man, did it feel good to be inside for a few minutes. Pretty much anything would have satisfied under those dismal circumstances, but the life-giving blend of caffeine and frothy warmth of the *cafe con leche* paired with the savory delights of *tortilla patata* was certainly a foretaste of the heavenly banquet. *Tortilla patata* is a kind of omelet on steroids. The eggs that serve as the scaffold for this pie-sized dish are lavishly supplemented by layers of thinly sliced potato, the combination of which is somehow—perhaps magically—both fluffy and dense. Variations contain mushrooms, vegetables, ham, or thickly sliced bacon. *Delicious* is such a weak, skinny word to describe this dish, which can be enjoyed at breakfast, lunch, dinner, or as a hearty snack. If served as a dessert I might ask for a second portion.

Tortilla patata. Manna from heaven.
(Tamorlan, CC BY-SA 3.0, via Wikimedia Commons)

We met Curt and Judy Robbins in the cafe. It would be our good fortune to see these friendly American pilgrims many times between Burguete and Santiago de Compostela. While on the pilgrim trail Curt and Judy go by "Mo and Flow." They were delightful conversationalists. I ought to amend this. As I think back on things, I do not recall Mo saying much at all. A handsome gentleman of perhaps sixty years, he tended to cede his podium time to his sweetie, who filled any crack or crevice in the conversation like sand fills a hole on the beach. Judy/Flow could—and did—talk about everything and anything. I always enjoyed seeing her coming down the trail, for a pleasant chat was sure to ensue.

It felt good to walk on reasonably flat ground from Burguete to Espinal, where we spent the night. Espinal was a tidy little village. Home to 250 souls, it was founded in the thirteenth century to protect pilgrims from bandits. After a difficult day of walking, we were certainly grateful for its protection. Albergue Irugoienea—a Basque word unpronounceable for all but the locals—was run by a young Sicilian couple, Zaira and Natale. They were a lovely pair who hosted us with selfless hospitality. After the usual check-in procedures Zaira showed us the house's bunkroom. I busied myself with sorting my wet items from the few things that stayed dry in anticipation of a long, hot shower. When I turned around, Craig had disappeared under a combination of sleeping bag and blanket, where he snored in contented slumber in the very clothing in which he had climbed the mountain. Could it be said that Craig "passed out?" I think it could. "Comatose" is adequately descriptive. For the briefest moment I worried if "deceased" was a possibility.

Zaira and Natale prepared a delicious home-cooked Italian meal for our fellow pilgrims and us. Craig and I ate like men truly starving, though the Irish ladies at our table did not think the cuisine up to their standards. Just pass your plates, ladies, and we'll be happy to clean them.

We met Laura—a second-year medical student from Bern, Switzerland. She was walking alone during a two-month break from her studies. She was fluent in four languages that I could detect. She was a lovely young woman, but seemed a bit unsure about her vocation. She was not doing as well as she would like in her courses, and was considering changing to a different program. I hope she was able to achieve the clarity she desired during her pilgrimage. She was a good reminder of what a privilege it is to serve as a professor for college students—another thing for which I was exceedingly grateful.

Chapter 4

Espinal to Zabaldica[1]

May I not rejoice in anything unless it leads me to You;
may I not be saddened by anything unless it turns me from You.
— Aquinas, Aquinas Prayer Book

JOE—MY 2016 pilgrim partner—was a slow, deliberate, careful packer in the morning. He carefully folded each article of clothing, inserted it in its own plastic bag, and lovingly placed the item into just the right place in his pack with a precision that reflected his expertise as a professional engineer. Watching Joe pack in the morning was like watching a priest handle the Sacrament. I, by way of comparison, shoved my clothes into one stuff sack, my gear into another, and both into an industrial strength garbage bag. The whole kit and kaboodle was jammed without fanfare into my backpack. Done. I learned to be cheerfully patient by pilgriming with Joe. Things were different with Craig in 2019. He was almost always ready before I was. I honestly do not know how he pulled this off. I was 97 percent packed before going to bed. I guess Craig was 98 percent packed.

We awoke from a still-jet-lagged, thin slumber by 5:30. We crept through the house's still-quiet halls and rooms in an effort to avoid

---

1. This village is variously spelled "Zabaldica" and "Zabaldika." The name of the *albergue* is consistently spelled with a "k."

disturbing our fellow *peregrinos*. When we tried to leave the *albergue* we found the front door locked from the inside. A key was required to unlock the door. The key was nowhere to be found. No one else was awake for us to make inquiries. This seemed like a fire hazard. Fortunately, we found an unlocked patio door, escaped through the back of the house, and stole away through the dark, damp Espinal streets.

The walk that morning began with a climb over the Alto de Erro, which provided stunning views, but also a rocky, difficult descent into Zubiri. It took us almost four hours to climb and descend the mountain and get to that riverside village. It felt good to be on level ground again. We had not eaten yet and we were starving. We found a small bar chockablock with locals and shared a table with three gentlemen who had no English and whose Spanish might have been Basque. We communicated through hand signs. The oldest of the locals barely acknowledged me when I tossed my best Spanish in his direction. I was beginning to take it personally until I noticed that he did not respond to his neighbors' inquiries either. It turns out that he was as deaf as a fencepost. With all forgiven, and after a hearty breakfast of fried eggs, thick bacon, French fries, and *cafe con leche*, we pushed on along the riverside path for Zabaldica.

La Puente de Rabia (Rabies Bridge) in Zubiri. (Tothh417, Creative Commons, CC0 1.0 Universal Public Domain Dedication)

We ran into Flow and Mo again around Larrasoaña. Flow was chatting at volume with a young couple pushing a ten-month-old baby in a Burley all the way to Santiago. It made me contemplate where the border between "adventure" and "insanity" is irrevocably breached. Mom and Dad seemed pretty chipper about everything, and given the difficulty they certainly endured pushing that buggy over the Alto de Erro, I gave them a lot of credit.

The last climb of the day up to the church and *albergue* at Zabaldica was a near vertical goat path. We arrived to the warmest hospitality we had yet encountered. The *albergue* and church were run by the Sisters of the Society of the Sacred Heart[2]—the same order of nuns that taught my mom and aunts in Detroit and Chicago. When I told *Hermanas* Marisol and Marisum of my family's ties to their religious order they could not have been more pleased. Lovely, lovely ladies, those two. There was a Mass before the shared pilgrim meal. Father Joseph—a pilgrim-priest of Indonesian birth ministering in an Australian parish with whom we'd walked part of the day—was a concelebrant along with the local priest. I sat next to Fr. Joseph during dinner and enjoyed a wonderful conversation. He looked confused when I asked him if he was looking forward to concelebrating the Pilgrim Mass at the cathedral in Santiago de Compostela.

"Is such a thing possible?" he asked, his excitement rising.

"Absolutely," I replied. "Just email your bishop and ask him to send a note verifying your priestly status. When you get to the cathedral just check in with the sacristan and he'll set you up with vestments. There will be many other pilgrim-priests doing the same thing." I thought he would hug me in his enthusiasm for the possibility.

The Sisters of the Society of the Sacred Heart took good care of us in Zabaldica.

2. https://rscj.org/.

One of the most beautiful aspects of the Camino is the terrific trove of people who simultaneously share and supplement the personal insights made possible by such an extended opportunity for prayer, conversation, and reflection. We met three people in Zabaldica with whom we would walk from time to time all the way to Santiago de Compostela. Josh and Bianka were a Canadian couple walking the Camino with a good friend of theirs—Monika from Germany. These generous conversation partners turned out to be wonderful company as we slowly made our way west.

The evening in Zabaldica concluded with a thirty-minute prayer service in the church's loft. Craig was recruited to read Scripture from the book of Kings. Others read in Spanish, Catalan, and French. One of the wonderful things about the Zabaldika *albergue* was that it had nonbunked beds. A pilgrim learns to appreciate a bed without a ladder. That said, the hallway and stairway lights were motion-activated, and flickered on whenever anyone moved a muscle. The lights flashed on and off all night long like a cheap motel near the interstate. Ugh. Still, the day overflowed with blessings, and I was very grateful for each one.

Chapter 5

Zabaldica to Zariquiegui

May I desire to please no one, nor fear to displease anyone, but You.
— *Aquinas, Aquinas Prayer Book*

W E left Zabaldica at 6:30 under a clear, brightening sky. It was chilly, but very nice for walking. We reached the outskirts of Pamplona after perhaps an hour and stopped for a *cafe con leche*. We roamed around Pamplona's still-sleeping Old City where we ran into Paul from Quebec in front of the cathedral. A ten-time Camino veteran, he had a ukulele and played "Over the Rainbow" while a small crowd gathered around. It was fun. After a rest on the city's ancient ramparts, we headed back though the old part of town, purchasing cheese, chorizo, fresh bread, and fruit for a picnic lunch, which we enjoyed on a sun-drenched bench on the campus of the University of Navarre as Pamplonans of every age and station walked past while taking in the warming Sunday sunshine.

Craig seemed particularly taken by Pamplona's ancient walls, sense of history, cathedral, and overall Navarran vibe. I regret that we did not linger there longer so he could enjoy the first sizable city we'd yet encountered. This was one disadvantage of sleeping in nonstage towns, which are typically smaller with less cultural interest. But the day was young, so we pushed on.

The walk out of Pamplona brought me back to 2016. I remembered well the long, slow, steady, seven-mile climb up to the Alto de Perdon with its iconic forty windmills and Camino sculptures. Craig and I did not make the entire climb that day, choosing instead to stay in the small village of Zariquiegui just below the summit. I asked the *hospitalero* there for the proper pronunciation of the name of his fair village. He smiled coyly and told me that even Spaniards have trouble sounding it out. He told me the village's name. I repeated it back to him. He offered a slight correction. I repeated the correction back to him. He smiled in recognition of my linguistic mastery. By the time I had walked ten steps the town's name was once again gibberish in my mouth. To the best of my recollection, it was pronounced "Thar-ee-wee-eh-wee." More or less. One wonders why epic poems immortalizing the virtue of this place have not been handed down through the ages and taught to schoolchildren the world over.

We only walked about twelve miles that day, but the last couple of hours were uphill, so we were glad to arrive. The San Andres *albergue* was a comfortable place. We ate a nice dinner in its bar. Guess who we ran into outside the village church? No sooner did we begin to turn the corner when we encountered the dulcet tones of Flow and her sidekick Mo. I liked them more each time I saw them. Flow helped me practice the virtue of listening more and speaking less, for she knew how to carry a conversation.

It was chilly that night. I needed to sleep in all my clothes, tucked inside a sleeping sack, and covered by a thick blanket. The next day we were off for Cirauqui and the site of the famous pilgrim firecracker bombings that made Joe and I chuckle in 2016.[1]

I had a phone call with Carol that evening. The day was great, and filled with gratitude for good fortune I did not deserve, but my call with Carol was the best part. I missed her, and wished I could express it as well as John Clare could:

> I loved her lip her cheek her eye
> She cheered my midnight gloom
> A bonny rose 'neath God's own sky
> In one perennial bloom
> She lives 'mid pastures evergreen
> And meadows ever fair
> Each winter spring and summer scene
> The sweetest woman there

1. Ray, *Shape of My Heart*, 49.

She lives among the meadow floods
That foams and roars away
While fading hedgerows distant woods
Fade off to naked spray
She lives to cherish and delight
All nature with her face
She brought me joy morn noon and night
In that low lonely place.[2]

2. Clare, *Selected Poems*, 344.

Chapter 6

Zariquiegui to Cirauqui

May all transitory things, O Lord, be worthless to me
and may all things eternal be ever cherished by me.
—Aquinas, Aquinas Prayer Book

C RAIG and I made the climb to the Alto de Perdon with its iconic windmills and Camino sculptures under a clear, brightening sky. Pamplona
and its suburbs were illumined in the dark valley below. It was very cold and
windy at the top, so we snapped a few photos and scurried down the other
side of the mountain before we became part of the permanent displays on
the peak, frozen in place for time and eternity.

One of the Camino's
most recognizable
places with its
reminders of
pilgrimage from an
earlier age. (Birgitta
Hellman Magnusson,
CC BY-SA 4.0 via
Wikimedia Commons)

The descent from the Alto de Perdon is a steep, rocky path. It was on this stretch where I began to experience problems with blisters under my toenails. This has been a chronic problem for me, as my feet are far from the elegant appendages God intended them to be. Instead, I have come to think that He crafted my feet from spare parts He had on some dusty shelf in His heavenly workshop. If I spend too much time walking downhill, I am going to develop blisters under my toenails.

And then my toenails will eventually fall off.

I lost seven of these presumably necessary body parts during the pilgrimage. You will likely have this grotesque image in your head for some time after reading this. My deepest apologies. Pilgrimage has its gritty, earthy elements.

The rolling, green wheat fields were spangled with bright red poppies. Gorgeous. When Joe and I pilgrimed to St. James in 2016 the wheat had already been harvested, leaving the fields the color of mud puddles. There was a special kind of stark beauty to those endless vistas, but the verdant landscapes we experienced on this pilgrimage were a feast for the eyes.

Ten kilometers after leaving Zariquiegui we came to a significant Camino town—Puente la Reina (Queen's Bridge). This place is mentioned in the eleventh century *Codex Calixtinus* as the town where four routes from France join together to form a unified road leading to the shrine of St. James at Santiago de Compostela. Today the town is best known for its lovely ancient bridge, which was a welcome addition when it was built since it helped pilgrims and others avoid the dangers of the river crossing and unscrupulous intentions of scheming ferrymen.

How pilgrims get from here to there in Puente la Reina. (Iñaki LL, CC BY-SA 3.0, via Wikimedia Commons)

Puente la Reina has a lovely church—La Iglesia del Crucifijo—built by the Knights Templar in the twelfth century. We stopped to admire its unique fourteenth-century, Y-shaped crucifix and amazing retablo. Ancient village churches were strung all along The Way like pearls on a necklace. Sometimes we would linger awhile, offering prayers for our pilgrimage intentions (remember those thirty rocks I was carrying?). At other times we would simply marvel at the priceless religious art that adorned these terrifically old sanctuaries. In every case these interludes from walking provided both physical and spiritual refreshment.

**Unusual Y-shaped crucifix in Puente la Reina
and the Spanish stamp that bears its image.**

From time to time Craig and I were reminded that Spain as a political concept is less enduring and robust than we might have otherwise imagined. The Camino was littered with graffiti proclaiming the people's dissatisfaction with Madrid's centralized political and economic authority. There are a dozen or more active separatist movements in Spain. The Basque Country, for example, has a long history of significant cultural and linguistic differences from the rest of the Iberian Peninsula. Though the Basques' armed insurrection that characterized the mid-late twentieth century has seemingly calmed, the people tend to think of themselves as Basques first and Spaniards second—if at all. Catalonia is presently engaged in much political and social upheaval about the question of Catalan autonomy—or even sovereign independence. There have been huge demonstrations in

Barcelona in recent years in support of this movement. The context for this sense of regionalism is complex, and dates in a formal sense to 1833. It was at this time that a system of provinces administered by a governor appointed by Madrid was adopted in a new constitution. But as Paul Preston explains:

> Ancient forms of politics, social influence and patronage, *casiquismo* or clientelism, took precedence over any kind of modern political machinery, poisoning what falteringly developed as electoral politics and leaving the state underfinanced and weak, other than in its coercive capacity.[1]

The Spanish Civil War—a conflict that took place ninety years before our pilgrimage—was still alive in the collective memories of many Spaniards, especially those of middle age or older. But the origins of regional identity in Spain are, in fact, many centuries old, dating back to at least the unification of the country under Ferdinand and Isabella—the so-called Catholic Monarchs. Spanish democracy in the modern era can be characterized as young, fragile, and torn between notions of European progressivist culture and Spain's Catholic-influenced traditionalist roots. Foreign pilgrims like Craig and I did our best to adopt a posture of respectful listening when issues of Spanish identity, culture, and politics came up in conversation.

And not just Galicia . . . (Luis Miguel Bugallo Sánchez [Lmbuga], CC BY-SA 3.0, via Wikimedia Commons)

1. Preston, *People Betrayed*, 7.

After a twenty-one-kilometer day we ascended the winding streets of Cirauqui. This charming town's Basque name translates as "nest of vipers" which is not exactly what one might call a Chamber of Commerce brand. The town sits atop a hill and seemed to be bereft of any flat places. Many of the sidewalks had stairs carved into their margins. Tough on the knees, Cirauqui. Albergue Maralotx (pronounced *mahr-a-losh*) was delightful and served a delicious dinner to the pilgrims who lodged there that evening. We spent some time after our arrival/grooming/laundering routine enjoying a beer in the *albergue's* bar while engaged in a pick-up sticks battle royal.[2] Though Craig was a worthy competitor, Rich is the reigning champion of the Spanish Pick-Up Sticks League. Endorsement deals, much to my bitter disappointment, have not materialized.

We began to encounter familiar faces as our "pilgrim bubble" flowed westward. We shared the *albergue* in Cirauqui with Josh, Bianka, and Monika, whom we met in Zabaldica. Walking with people we met in earlier places along the Camino resulted in a pleasant spirit of developing friendship. Some who walk the Camino de Santiago begin to think of those with whom they peregrinate as part of an intimate Camino family. Some people who adopt—or are adopted into—such a family begin the pilgrimage alone, but soon connect with others who eventually influence their decisions about many things—where to stay, how far to walk, who to include in the group, where to eat, etc. It may be the case that self-described extroverts who draw their mental energy from deep engagements in social groups are more likely to join a Camino family. Introverts, on the other hand, find it exhausting to interact with others.[3] They can do it, but they don't enjoy it in the same way a pilgrim-extrovert might. When I use the term "pilgrim bubble" in this account of our journey, I do so with the express intention of seeking a middle ground between the overcharged enthusiasms of those craving the intimacy and subjugation of self-will to that of a Camino family and those quieter souls worn weary by having to put on a happy face around others. A pilgrim bubble is a loose association of people who, through patient, subtle tests, discover that they enjoy each other's company, who can imagine the possibility of friendship with others who happen to share their time and space along The Way, but who still prefer to walk their own Camino. There is a status and state for every pilgrim in this paradigm.

2. Pick-up sticks is a game also known as pick-a-stick, jackstraws, jack straws, spillikins, or spellicans.

3. Anonymous, "Introverted Pilgrim."

I enjoyed the pilgrim bubble of which Craig and I were a part, but I was beginning to miss my real family. I love being a pilgrim, but my vocation is certainly ordered toward hearth and home, kith and kin. Carol and I would be reunited in about one month, and it could not come too soon. The longer I spent away from her, the more grateful I was for the blessings of our marriage.

Chapter 7

Cirauqui to Villamayor de Monjardín

*May any joy without You be burdensome for me
and may I not desire anything else besides You.*
— Aquinas, Aquinas Prayer Book

THE day was wonderful for walking. The skies were slightly overcast and the temperatures were comfortable—at least until the last hour of the walk when things warmed up. Still, as I sat writing my notes in the evening I needed long pants and a jacket.

There were four distinct chapters to the walk between Cirauqui and Villamayor de Monjardín. Not every day falls into such neat categories, but a pilgrimage is a strange and wonderful phenomenon. As soon as you think you understand it—as soon as it becomes predictable—the day will surprise you.

The first chapter of my walk on that day was a deep, surprisingly intense focus on whether I'd been sufficiently grateful for the ways that God healed me during and after my first pilgrimage in 2016. I was a wreck before undertaking that Camino journey. I was not yet sixty years of age and I had no idea what vocation to which I was being called after losing my role as a senior administrative leader at the college where I've taught for nearly four decades. And it was not for lack of listening for God's voice. I prayed every day for the grace to know what to do with the final stage of my career. The 2016 Camino was an extension of that divine conversation. While I spent lots of time talking with Joe, I also devoted that walk to a prayerful plea for some degree of clarity regarding what I should do with whatever time I had left in this life. I was also seeking the grace to be able to forgive certain people with whom I was very angry for my professional demise. While I cannot say that I walked into the Praza do Obradoiro in front of the Santiago cathedral that October with a roadmap for the rest of my life, I can testify that I received the grace I needed to simply and honestly say "Here I am Lord. Send me."

And send me He has.

I've never been happier with the teaching I'm privileged to do with my students. I can see the promise and possibilities in my students in ways that generate fresh appreciation for their deep humanity. And not just the best students either. Even those who require all the extra help and attention I can give them—the really complicated students—even they bring me joy in ways that haven't always been the case. The work I have been privileged to undertake to plant a college degree in one of our local prisons since returning from my first pilgrimage has been like a Damascus Road experience for me. A gift of great price.

One can never be grateful enough for undeserved blessings. But during that day's walk I vowed that I would do my very best to avoid taking for granted the ways my life had been turned around. Medieval pilgrims often undertook their journeys in fulfillment of a vow. I now felt a certain kinship with them.

Church of the Holy Sepulcher in Jerusalem. Pilgrims in bygone times often made their pilgrimages in fulfillment of a religious vow for the salvation of their souls— often to this shrine. (Rijksmuseum, CC0, via Wikimedia Commons)[1]

1. Davies, *Bernhard Von Breydenbach*, ii.

The second chapter of that day's walk was characterized by the wonderful conversation Craig and I enjoyed with fellow pilgrims Josh, Bianka, and Monika. We first encountered these three fellow-travelers in the *albergue* at Zabaldica. Since then we'd seen them here and there, but today we had the chance to walk a long distance with them, learning more about their lives, and discussing a wide range of subjects of mutual interest. Josh was a consultant to engineers and architects on how to design their buildings in more energy-efficient ways. While he and Bianka are Canadians, Monika is a German who used to work with Josh before he started his own consulting firm. Still, their friendship remained firm and they seemed to be enjoying each other's company during this pilgrimage. All three were younger than us and were very fit. Each walked at a brisk pace, but Bianka was the gold medalist in this category. She was very kind to slow down for our conversations. I am pleased to say that I have been able to stay in occasional contact with all three of these new friends since finishing the Camino.

Chapter three of the day's pilgrimage took place just past the village of Ayegui at one of the Camino's signature memory-makers: the Irache wine fountain. This place is rather famous among pilgrims to St. James. It sits adjacent to a winery that is connected to a Benedictine monastery dedicated to Santa Maria de Real.[2] Pilgrims may help themselves to water or wine. I have been to this place twice and never seen anyone even jiggle the tap on the water spigot. I'm confident that a survey of pilgrims would reveal complete ignorance that water is available at Irache. While Craig had spent lots of time before our pilgrimage prepping for the sights he would encounter, he must have looked past this delicious tidbit.

"What's this place?" he asked as we climbed the gentle slope leading to the fountain, noting the gaggle of pilgrims huddled around something he still didn't understand.

"Free wine," I responded.

"No way," said Craig, incredulous.

"Honest. All you can drink. Belly up to the bar."

Well, the image below tells the rest of the story. It's a good thing scallop shells have shallow bottoms or we'd still be there.

---

2. The Irache monastery dates back at least as far as 958, and may even be from Visigothic times. It hosted a Benedictine university from the seventeenth to the early nineteenth century, and offered degrees in philosophy, canon law, letters, medicine, and theology (Gitlitz and Davidson, *Pilgrimage Road to Santiago,* 108–9).

Craig enjoys his free wine.

The day's fourth chapter is an *albergue* story. The *albergue* experience is one of the most enjoyable aspects of the Camino pilgrimage. Discerning readers may reasonably demand evidence to defend this unlikely assertion. How could anyone claim that sleeping in a bunk bed—perhaps on the top bunk, connected to *terra firma* by only a rickety ladder, sharing a toilet and shower, and listening to the nightly emanations of a dozen strangers—could be described as enjoyable? Well, as it turns out, it is the *strangers* that make the experience enjoyable. The Hogar de Monjardín (House of the Garden on the Hill) *albergue* was a perfect example. This hostelry was operated by a group of retired Dutch *hospitaleros* who volunteer a couple of weeks of their time each summer to extend hospitality to pilgrims. Such *albergues* sponsored by national associations are commonplace along the Camino. This *albergue* was part of a larger network of hostels called Oasis Trails. The Dutch group who hosted us had a religious mission rooted in providing hospitality to strangers. And such hospitality! Francis, Ellie, Joop, Jan, and their friends met us at the door and provided us with a refreshing beverage and snack. They eased the minds of those who feared that they wouldn't get a bed by assuring them that they would move heaven and earth to see them suitably lodged. I live in a town founded by Dutch immigrants known for their orderliness, cleanliness, and sense of reserved propriety. I felt like I had come home as we settled in at the Hogar de Monjardín. Arriving pilgrims were arranged by time of arrival and reservation status. They were admitted one at a time at precisely 1:00, and not one minute earlier. We were fed a delightful meal at 6:00, and were invited to an ecumenical prayer service at 8:00. It was lights out at 9:00. The combination of the welcome, the meal, and the shared prayer had a kind of magical effect in drawing thirty people who didn't know each other into a group of people who—at least for a little while—cared for each other. *Albergue* life—done right—is wonderful.

This chapter in that day's journey deserves further comment. Do you remember the first time (or the hundredth?) as a child when your mother warned you to be wary of strangers? "Don't talk to strangers," she chided. We kids *learned* to suspect and even anticipate the worst in others. We were not born this way. Our parents—in an effort to keep us safe, protected, whole, and healthy—conditioned us to be suspicious about others' intentions. Did I do the very same thing with my own children? Indeed, I did. But my Camino experiences have taught me to fight against this conditioning. I have encountered such undeserved kindness from others on the pilgrimage that I gradually began to understand that *strangers are good.* People I did not know were willing to talk to me. People I did not know were kind to me. People I did not know acted in ways that reflected the fundamental goodness of their humanity. One or two people disappointed me, but they were obvious outliers. The Camino taught me that if I expect the best from others, I'm more likely than not to get their best. The Camino reminded me of C.S. Lewis's understanding of people:

> There are no ordinary people. You have never talked to a mere mortal. . . . It is immortals whom we joke with, work with, marry, snub, and exploit. . . . Next to the Blessed Sacrament itself, your neighbor is the holiest object presented to your senses.[3]

I came to expect the best from every person I encountered on the Camino. And this attitude—this way of being—has carried forward to my life after the Camino. No one wants to be unsafe. No one seeks to be hurt. No one desires injury, pain, or unkindness. But our conditioned desire to be safe shackles us and prevents us from being the best version of ourselves. Family and friends tend to be hamstrung in teaching us this lesson. Their felt obligation to love us tends to shelter us from the point of view that ultimately sets us free. Only strangers can teach us this truth. Family and friends present us with hypotheses. Strangers present us with proven facts. Strangers, it turns out, are important for our flourishing. Strangers are good.

This point of view is not merely a dreamy, romantic reminiscence that occurs to me nearly two years after the pilgrimage. Scholars of pilgrimage recognize the bonding of strangers along the pilgrim's way as a form of

3. Lewis, *Weight of Glory*, 46.

communitas. Consider the views of British cultural anthropologist Victor Turner:

> *Communitas* emerges in the liminal (a kind of spiritual threshold) stages of pilgrimages. *Communitas* means relationships among people, jointly undergoing ritual transition, through which they experience an intense sense of intimacy and equality, an 'I-Thou' awareness. *Communitas* is spontaneous, immediate, concrete . . . undifferentiated, egalitarian, direct, non-rational . . .[4]

Some may think this attitude—this conviction that strangers are good—is the very height of naivete. It is true that I have lived a life of privilege. The neighborhoods in which I have lived have been orderly, calm, and reasonably free of violence. Others who have been less fortunate might criticize the notion that strangers are good because of the hard knocks to which they have been subjected. I will not try to gainsay them here. Their experiences have worth. But important, too, is hope. It has been said that despair is the unforgivable sin.[5] Despair is the sense that "God is on leave."[6] Despair robs the despairing of any imagination that things can be better. To despair is to deny God's omnipotence, his presence in others. Call me naive, but I would rather be called hopeful. God is not on leave, but present to all who seek Him earnestly. And speaking of God, I am aware that not everyone I met on the Camino—indeed, not everyone who reads these words—believes in God, much less *loves* Him. But I do, and a big part of my assertion that strangers are good comes from this:

> Beloved, we love God because
> He first loved us.
> If anyone says, "I love God,"
> but hates his brother, he is a liar;
> for whoever does not love a brother whom he has seen
> cannot love God whom he has not seen. (1 John 4:19–20)

The students in my Senior Seminar at Hope College are required to write a capstone paper in which they are expected to commit to paper their worldviews. My own worldview convinces me that St. Augustine had the closest understanding of how people are put together. We human beings, he asserts, are principally *creatures of desire.* Our hearts—not our heads—are

4. Turner, *Dramas, Fields, and Metaphors,* 274.
5. Snell, "Quiet Hope," 8.
6. Wiesenthal, *Sunflower,* 6.

the first drivers of our thoughts, actions, and habits. If he is right—if we are not merely *thinking things*[7]—then understanding the deepest desire of our hearts is a critical step in understanding ourselves. Toward this end, my students are asked to answer five questions:

- What do you want (or desire, love, worship)?

- Why do you want it?

- Is the thing you say you want what you are likely to want at the very end of your life?

- How will you know when you have obtained the thing you want?

- How will others know what you want?

To help the students organize their thinking for this significant task, I provide them with my worldview paper. And in that essay they will read the following reflection on desire, which this Camino caused me to amend in its final stanza:

ON DESIRE

If my deepest desire is money, I'll always feel poor.

If my deepest desire is power, I'll never feel in control.

If my deepest desire is for material goods, the things I have will never satisfy.

If my deepest desire is to be loved, I'll always fear rejection.

If my deepest desire is to be attractive, I'll always feel ugly.

If my deepest desire is to be thin, I'll always feel fat.

If my deepest desire is to live a long life, I'll always fear death.

If my deepest desire is to be popular, I'll always walk alone.

If my deepest desire is perfect health, aches and pains will be my constant companions.

If my deepest desire is a perfect world, the daily headlines will haunt me.

If my deepest desire is for many friends, I'll find myself surrounded by those who don't really know me.

If my deepest desire is to follow my own heart, I'll live life closed off to others.

If my deepest desire is to be successful, I'll never be truly grateful for the good things I have but do not deserve.

If my deepest desire is to be safe, I'll never see the face of God in the face of a stranger.

Strangers are good.

7. Smith, *You Are What You Love*, 3.

Strangers becoming friends around a shared pilgrim's meal. (Henri Bergius from
Finland, CC BY-SA 2.0, via Wikimedia Commons)

There is one more anecdote to share about our afternoon in Villamayor
de Monjardin. The *albergue* sits on the slope of a hill, with the Romanesque
Iglesia de San Andrés an easy five-minute walk away. Craig and I noted
some activity at the church when the belfry's bells began to sound even
though it was neither the hour nor the half-hour. Craig thought he would
take a stroll down to the church to check on the commotion. I had been
down to the church earlier in the afternoon. Being pleasantly planted in a
shady spot, I couldn't be bothered with further investigation. After forty-
five minutes or so I began to wonder what became of Craig. A few minutes
later he came ambling up the lane with what can only be described as a
spring in his step.

"Where have you been?" I inquired.

"Well," he replied with growing excitement, "Today is my lucky day.
There is a funeral in the church!"

He went on to describe the event in microscopic, breathless detail.
Take my advice. If you die, call Craig. No one will sweat the details as he
can. No one.

Chapter 8

Villamayor de Monjardín
to Viana

May all work, O Lord, delight me when done for Your sake and may all repose
not centered in You be ever wearisome for me.
— Aquinas, Aquinas Prayer Book

I T was difficult to avoid tallying up the miles as we made our way slowly west. My view was that such mile-minding distracts from the most human elements of the pilgrimage, and renders it a kind of transactional experience. Mile-counting is a bit like clock-watching. Miles seem longer and less pleasant when counted, just as time seems to drag when we check the clock too often. Regrettably, the Camino is littered with signage of every type alerting pilgrims to their progress. We had walked 150 kilometers so far. I wished I had not known this, but I did.

It's hard to avoid mile-counting on the Camino.
(José Antonio Gil Martínez from Vigo, Spain, CC
BY 2.0, via Wikimedia Commons)

So averse am I to mile-counting that I spoke to Craig about this as we prepared for the journey. He was understandably concerned about walking 500 miles. This was, after all, a very long walk. A lot can go wrong. Blistered, infected feet. Shin splints. Dodgy knees and hips. Illnesses of various kinds. Crippling kidney stones. Encounters with wild animals. Rabid dogs and mad cows. Hypothermia. Dehydration and heat stroke. Lightning strikes. You name it, it can happen. I encouraged Craig to think one day at a time. Indeed, even smaller segments would be preferable.

"Think of each day's walk as a pleasant amble from the *albergue* to a delicious breakfast of *cafe con leche* and *tortilla patata*, *tostada*, or *empanada*. Thus fortified, imagine next walking from that place to a delightful park down the track a bit, where we'll make sandwiches with fresh, crusty bread adorned with the finest produce in the land. Following this delicious repast we may even enjoy a brief rest in a leafy glade or sun-dappled meadow. Then it's on to *Cafe Con Leche* Stop Number Two. We'll be there before you know it, so varied and interesting will be the landscape, the people, and fascinating towns and villages. And within an hour or two of this energy-booster we will arrive in the village-of-the-day, where we'll be received like royal dignitaries and presented with the keys to the city."

Craig looked suspicious when I suggested adopting this frame of mind. Five hundred miles, 500 schmiles is my philosophy. I'm simply walking to my next meal.

The walk between Villamayor de Monjardin and Viana took us through Los Arcos, Sansol, and Torres del Río. The first stretch was about twelve kilometers through empty countryside, which made for hungry, thirsty walking until we could find breakfast. We spent most of the day walking with Monika. It was fun getting to know her better, learning about her home in Ludwigsburg near Stuttgart, and the good work she was doing in the Green Energy sector.

Los Arcos is a common stage town for many pilgrims. We walked through it during mid-morning. It was an interesting place with a terrific church—Iglesia de Santa María de la Asunción, which was constructed over a 600-year period, though little remains of the original structure.[1] Here's what the guidebook had to say about Los Arcos:

> Los Arcos occupies an ideal location by the Río Odrón and at the crossroads of two ancient trade routes, and was once a Roman city (Curnonium). The current name comes from a battle in 914 when

1. Gitlitz and Davidson, *Pilgrimage Road to Santiago,* 114.

three Sanchos (the kings of Navarra, Castilla and Aragon) fought over the town. The Navarran army won with the help of their excellent archers, therefore the coat of arms of the city contains bows (arcos) and arrows. In medieval times, the city was a place for toll collection and changing money. Los Arcos flourished as a market town, becoming quite wealthy with all this pilgrim commerce.[2]

While this account ascribes the town's name change to the success of Navarran arms, I do not think we should so blithely reject the possibility that the city's poo-bahs were concerned about being confused with one of the metallic elements, like Europium, Samarium, or even Ytterbium. This makes sense to me, for I would hate to wander into Curnonium thinking I'd lost my way and had stumbled unawares into radioactive Ytterbium.

Iglesia de Santa María de la Asunción, Los Arcos.

I found myself running low on cash between Cirauqui and Villamayor de Monjardín. No problem. There are cash machines in many towns along The Way. I stopped at one, inserted my card, and was disappointed to

2. Harms et al., *Camino de Santiago*, 221.

receive an error message. Hmmm. I tried a second time. Same message. Perhaps, I thought to myself, the machine is faulty. I'll just try a different one. Five minutes later we found another bank with an ATM. Insert card. Error message. "No problem" turned into "problem." Craig lent me some cash and I sent Carol a WhatsApp text alerting her to the issue and asking her to check with the bank back home. She came through like a champ, and as we walked through Los Arcos I was able to successfully withdraw some cash, repay Craig, and stop worrying that I might have to sing for my supper as we pilgrimed along.

One of the best things about the Camino—and this follows Principle 1: Strangers Are Good—is trying to communicate with fellow pilgrims in whatever language may be common to both parties. While English has become the *lingua franca* in many parts of the world—the Camino included—not everyone could speak to Craig and me in our native language. I can speak a bit of Spanish, but only a bit. Any attempt at extended conversation necessitating complex ideas and I may as well be speaking Martian. Just past Los Arcos we ran into a one-thumbed fellow from Lithuania. Man, we could not communicate with each other—not one bit. Still, we tried. Smiles go a long way on the Camino. We would run into this pilgrim later on—in Astorga—after we found a wallet with a Lithuanian driver's license. As it turns out, there must have been more than one Lithuanian on the Camino in our general vicinity, for the wallet was not the property of the one-thumbed fellow.

The day was lovely for walking. It was overcast for the most part, but the breeze kicked up as we approached Viana. On balance I must admit to some surprise at the generally chilly weather we experienced on the Camino. The second day at the top of the Pyrenees was just downright miserably cold, but for at least the first 400 miles of our walk I cannot recall being hot and sweaty. There were some warmish days after that, but I never regretted my long pants, fleece jacket, or wool cap. And most days' walks were under clear, blue skies. We had some clouds and a couple of drizzly moments, but most days were great.

We met Priscilla strolling along toward Viana, a seventysomething gal from Tasmania. She was a real sweetheart who by her own admission walked very slowly, took her time, and could not be bothered with her rate of forward progress. A traveling "bush nurse" during her working years, she told us a funny story. Earlier in the day she sat down on a concrete ledge near a ditch and tipped ass-over-apple-cart right into the water. She laughed it off as if this kind of thing happened all the time. What a lovely lady.

After a thirty-kilometer stroll we sidled into our home for the night: Viana. The last bit of the path between Torres Del Río and Viana was up and down and up again. It felt like a lot of work, and we were happy to arrive.

Iglesia de Santa María de la Asunción in Viana is where cardinal-turned-warrior Cesare Borgia is buried. He was the illegitimate soldier son of Rodrigo Borgia, a.k.a. Pope Alexander VI. That guy gave popes a bad name for a long time. Some scholars think that the image of Jesus as a white, European, made-for-TV figure is based on the ruggedly handsome visage of Cesare Borgia. *History Today* has this to say about Viana's most interesting tourist attraction:

> Brave, daring and determined, he was insatiably power-hungry and entirely ruthless. Murder, bribery and deceit were all in the day's work to him and his pleasures were women, hunting and fashionable clothes. He was considered the handsomest man in Italy, there were inevitably rumors of incest with his sister Lucrezia and he had syphilis from his early twenties.[3]

Cesare's syphilitic couplings with his sister notwithstanding, the church that hosts his final resting place is fantastic. We enjoyed a stroll through its dimmed aisles while the grandmas of the town scurried about like an army of sweepers and dusters, tidying the place up.

Cesare Borgia[4] and his no-good, very bad, scoundrel of a father, Pope Alexander VI. (Giovanni Battista Gaulli, Public domain, via Wikimedia Commons)

3. Cavendish, "Death of Cesare Borgia," 2.

4. By Altobello Melone. Bergamo, Accademia Carrara. 1500–24.

Our *albergue* offered a shared pilgrim dinner which was great. The meal was prepared with kindness and served with generosity by the *hospitaliteros*. Following dinner Craig and I retired to the rooftop patio to allow our meal some time to settle. It was a nice setting in which to write in my journal, catch up on messages from home, and offer a prayer of thanksgiving for the blessings of the day. I had much for which to be grateful, as I do even up to the present time.

The next day I would turn sixty-two. I decided to mark the occasion with a twenty-kilometer walk.

Chapter 9

Viana to Navarrete

You arouse us so that praising you may bring us joy, because you have made us and drawn us to yourself, and our heart is restless until it rests in you.

—ST. AUGUSTINE[1]

T HE morning—and the sixty-second anniversary of my birth—came quickly. We were on the road by 6:00. Goodbye, Cesare Borgia. Goodbye, Viana and your 4,000 souls. God bless you, everyone.

It was a perfect morning for walking, with clear skies, cool temperatures, and a light breeze. The path was gentle with only one mild *alto* between Logroño and Navarrete. We walked from Viana to Logroño with Claude from Quebec and Marianne from France. Both were in our *albergue* in Viana. Marianne's English was very thin, though we could communicate a bit. Both she and Claude were recently retired teachers, and thus had plenty to discuss of mutual interest. I did not have to talk much because Claude proved very capable in that department. A very nice fellow indeed.

---

1. Augustine, Confessions, 1.

Puente de Piedra (Stone Bridge) over the Rio Ebro into Logroño.
(jynus, Creative Commons Attribution Share Alike 3.0)

As we entered Logroño—the capital of the autonomous region of La Rioja—we were charmed by the rooftop stork nests with their huge occupants nursing the soon-to-be-huge chicks. I bet we saw seven or eight nests in all as we scanned Logroño's skyline. It is considered very good luck to have a stork nest on your roof, chimney, or church belfry. If this is true, then the La Rioja region was a most auspicious place.

The storks we encountered built their nests in some precarious places. (Zeynel Cebeci, CC BY-SA 4.0 via Wikimedia Commons)

Storks are, of course, the subject of much folklore around the world. Myths centered on the various virtues of storks include:

- Good fortune: when storks arrive and linger, good luck follows, and bad fortune is associated with their departure;

- Family values: storks provide examples of loyalty among spouses, fealty to parents, and devotion to and care of children;

- Christian faith: storks were reputedly present at both the birth and death of Jesus, providing feathers to soften the rough wood of the manger and words of comfort during his passion on the cross;

- Fellow travelers with the human soul: many cultures and religious traditions hold that storks journey with the human soul during important transitions, including birth and death. This may be why storks are thought to be auspicious agents of fertility. Parents across the world through the ages have explained to their children that a stork would soon bring a new baby to the family home.[2]

Our entrance into Logroño also marked our exit from Navarre. We would spend the next few days walking through the wine country of La Rioja, known the world over for its *vin extraordinaire*. We felt a certain sense of accomplishment in having traversed an entire autonomous region of a big, sprawling country.

The huge church in Logroño[3] was open, so we stopped in to admire its fantastic altarpiece and other works of art. I offered my morning prayers there for my family and all those whose stones I was carrying on this pilgrimage.

The walk out of Logroño is along a two-to-three-mile linear park that includes a lovely lake, picnic areas, and wooded paths. It was a delightful place to stop, enjoy an orange and a candy bar, air feet, and take in Logroño's citizens enjoying this wonderful public amenity. We spoke with a couple of retired gents who were having some luck pulling fish after fish from the lake. They claimed that the fish were trout, but they did not look like any kind of trout with which I was familiar. Perhaps they were *trucha d'España*, rarely observed in Michigan waterways.

As we relaxed at a picnic table Josh, Bianka, and Monika walked by and we exchanged greetings and news of the day. They were pushing on to

2. Watts, "Stork," 897–98.

3. An ironic historical fact of the La Rioja region is that the oldest churches in this part of Spain were financed with Islamic funds paid as *parias* (tribute) to prevent Christian armies from destroying their territories (Gitlitz and Davidson, *Pilgrimage Road to Santiago*, 144).

Ventosa that day, while we planned to quit in Navarrete. We were not sure if we would see them again, but we hoped we would, for we enjoyed their company.

We picked up a few groceries for lunch from a small shop as we entered Navarrete, which would be our home for the evening. We used these to make a late picnic lunch in the town square in front of the church.

Navarrete is not New York City. Home to a mere 2,900 people, there is not much going on there. It once had a castle, but it is long-gone. Navarrete is considered a "pottery center" which no doubt stirs the imagination. Navarrete may be a forgettable place, but its church is unforgettable. The altarpiece is simply impossible to describe except to say that it is a massive study in gold. And I mean massive.

Spain—like other early-modern powers—grew its sphere of influence around the globe in the fifteenth through nineteenth centuries, exporting approximately 2 million citizens to conquer new lands and establish Christianity among peoples considered less civilized. But Spain was not just in the exporting business. It was also interested in importing from these new lands. Spices were in demand back home. So was gold. The Spanish obsession with finding and "liberating" gold from the Americas for King and Country eventually led to the legend of El Dorado, a golden city hidden deep in the jungle high up in the mountains. While the Spanish never found El Dorado, they did bring home a considerable quantity of gold. Between 1500 and 1650, the Spanish imported 181 tons of gold and 16,000 tons of silver from the New World.[4] Some of that gold found its way onto the altarpiece of Navarrete's Iglesia de La Asunción. Craig and I gladly popped a one-euro coin into the box at the rear of the church that caused the *retablo* to be illuminated for five minutes. It was five minutes and one euro well-spent.

4. Taylor, American Colonies, 63.

Navarrete *retablo*. My God.

We made a reservation for the next day in Cirueña, thirty-one kilometers from Navarrete. It would be our longest day so far. I hoped my knees and feet would hold up.

As I said my prayers and laid down to sleep, I gave thanks for the gift of sixty-two years. May 9, 2019 was a good birthday. That said, I was beginning to feel the absence of my family. As much as I enjoy exploring the world, I'm just not made to be away from them for too long. Still, the consolation offered by Charles Dickens reassured me as I drifted off to sleep:

"The pain of parting is nothing to the joy of meeting again."[5]

5. Dickens, *Nicholas Nickleby*, 41.

Chapter 10

Navarrete to Cirueña

Grant unto me, my God, that I may direct my heart to You and that in my failures I may ever feel remorse for my sins and never lose the resolve to change.
— Aquinas, Aquinas Prayer Book

E L Cantaro was a nice place by *albergue* standards, but the dorm room was very warm and stuffy in the night. It felt good to get up, get dressed, and get going at 5:45 in the cool morning air. As small as Navarrete was, the *albergue* was a bit off the Camino route, and we stumbled around trying to figure out how to get out of town.

Navarrete held some charming elements, like this ancient portico. (Pigmentoazul, CC BY-SA 4.0 via Wikimedia Commons)

The day's walk was very rural and took us through many (many!) vine-yards and wheat fields. We stopped for coffee and Napoleons in Ventosa. Coffee and pastries after a brisk six-mile walk tasted very nice.

We stopped for a sock change on a sidewalk bench in Nájera.[1] An ancient man came shuffling past, stopped in front of us as he scanned the hill he had to climb, and sighed. I gave him a dose of my best Spanish and we had a nice chat. I believe he told me that he was ninety years old, and had four children and seven grandchildren. Between them they only had one car. Because the others needed the car to get to work, Grandpa had to walk. He seemed resigned to his fate, and toddled gamely along.

If I had a car I would have given this fellow a lift. (Adam Jones from Kelowna, BC, Canada, CC BY-SA 2.0 , via Wikimedia Commons)

Farther along on our walk through Nájera we came upon Katje, a twentysomething German pilgrim whom we had seen from time to time. She looked distressed and asked if either of us knew anything about back-packs. She was having a difficult time getting hers adjusted. Her neck and shoulders were in rough shape as a result. We showed her how to get the pack riding on her hips and she seemed better. We would see Katje from time to time through the middle third of the pilgrimage, but then she disap-peared from our pilgrim bubble.

1. The basis of most Spanish law can be traced to principles enshrined in the *fuero* (charter) issued to Nájera by King Sancho Garcés III *"El Mayor"* in the eleventh century (Gitlitz and Davidson, *Pilgrimage Road to Santiago,* 135).

I saw many unusual sights on our pilgrimage. Parents toting infants. Blind pilgrims. Pilgrims in wheelchairs. But in the 1,000 miles I have walked through Spain I had not yet encountered a golfing pilgrim. As I was minding my own business along the dusty path between Nájera and Azofra I looked up and noticed Craig walking perhaps 100 yards ahead of me. Next to him was a man strolling along with a golf club. Craig was attempting to engage the man in conversation, though it did not seem as if he was getting much of a verbal response from this fellow traveler, as he had no English. He carried no pack, no water—nothing but a single golf club. We entered Azofra and never saw him again.

Craig and I settled into a routine of stopping at neighborhood shops (in villages) or grocery stores (in larger cities) to purchase ingredients for a simple lunch, which we normally ate in a park or town square. We often made sandwiches. Craig began to tire of chorizo as the principal element of our noon repast, so we vowed to move through all of the various proteins as alternatives. The choice as we lunched in Azofra was tuna. Yum. A mandarin orange and a lemon cookie rounded out the meal nicely. I know, I know. A tuna sandwich, an orange, and a cookie does not seem especially newsworthy. The fact that I am reporting it here should give you an idea of how pilgriming has long periods where very little happens to occasion comment. On some days a tuna sandwich was a headline story.

The last ten kilometers to Cirueña was uphill, boring, and loooong. Honestly, it was a slog. But slogs have the benefit of being good opportunities for prayer. I did my best to take advantage of stretches like this to pray the rosary, offer prayers for friends and family, and reflect on God's grace bestowed so generously on me, despite my unworthiness.

With sincere apologies to those who call it home, Cirueña was a miserable, haunted place, and gave new meaning to the term *of mean estate*. The newer part of the village consisted of an eerily empty housing development which went bust when the global economy tanked in 2008. It was weird walking through street after street of vacant homes. I imagined that there were great deals to be had if you did not mind living alone in a ghost town. The old part of the village was tiny—with a population of less than 150. It was unforgettable in every respect, and merely a place to sleep for the night. Cirueña could be likened to Charlie Brown's Christmas tree—in need of lots of love.

We were very glad to arrive at the *albergue*, which we shared with several pilgrims who would be part of our bubble much of the way to

Santiago de Compostela. Rainbow was an artist from Pennsylvania. Katje from earlier in the day also joined us in Cirueña. We were introduced to the peripatetic Mags from Perth, Australia, who always had her backpack shipped ahead to the next day's destination. George from Hungary had limited English, and since I spoke no Hungarian (or German) we struggled to communicate with each other. Finally, Lu from Japan dragged in later in the afternoon. He was an interesting guy with whom we would have many conversations as the pilgrimage progressed. We spoke at length in Cirueña about his experience as a Henro pilgrim on Japan's famous eighty-eight-temple Shikoku pilgrimage, about which I teach in my Senior Seminar.

We were grateful for the delicious shared meal prepared by the *hospitalera*. It provided a nice opportunity to interact with the other pilgrims sharing the Albergue Victoria. We took a stroll around the village after dinner, but there was nothing to see but crumbling buildings and a shuttered church. The guidebook alleges that 142 people live here, but they must have all decided to go on vacation at the same time.

Chapter 11

Cirueña to Viloria de la Rioja

O Lord my God, make me submissive without protest.
— Aquinas, Aquinas Prayer Book

P EOPLE who are interested in, or perhaps planning for, their own Camino pilgrimage can be fooled into the idea that the skies over Spain are always a deep, cerulean blue, that the purpose of clouds is to provide dreamy poets a subject for their romantic verse, that the path is broad and soft underfoot, containing no stones, and never muddy. Well, it is certainly true that Northern Spain offers many atmospheric delights, but it does rain from time to time. The walk between Cirueña and Grañon was our chance to be reminded of this cruel but necessary fact. We did not get soaked, but were never completely dry either—at least during the early part of the walk.

As we beat a hasty exit from Cirueña I was reminded that back home in Holland, Michigan my friends and neighbors would be celebrating our fair city's 175-year-old Dutch heritage. The annual Tulip Time festival is a two-week series of musical events, street food, flower shows, and parades. Hundreds of thousands of tourists render the town unnavigable as streets are jammed with tour busses and overflowing with bewildered motorists seeking parking, and all while closed roads are turned into entertainment venues. Carol and I live downtown near the hubbub and are much

A damp morning for pilgriming as we passed from La Rioja into our third region—Castilla y León.

disadvantaged in our daily movements during this otherwise festive time. I grew a bit homesick for it all as Craig and I dodged the mud puddles on the way to Santo Domingo de la Calzada and beyond.

The Way was an empty, lonely place during the first couple of hours of our walk. The farther west we walked the greater the distance between population centers, or so it seemed to us as our stomachs rumbled, demanding breakfast. Eventually we rounded a bend while ascending a low hill and came to an apparently new wayside park and modernist sculpture dedicated to the millennial anniversary of the founding of the town of Santo Domingo de la Calzada, which now greeted us on the horizon.

There were more pilgrims as we entered and through Santo Domingo de la Calzada. That place is a stage town in most guidebooks, so we wondered if people were resting there and spilling out onto the path after their evening's recuperation in the large *albergue* run by the ancient *Cofradía del Santo*—established in 1106 to extend hospitality to pilgrims. Or perhaps pilgrims who'd done their homework better than Craig and I timed their passage through this town during its 1000-year-anniversary celebration. Who knows?

Santo Domingo de la Calzada is named for St. Dominic of the Highway, an eleventh-century Benedictine monk who labored on behalf of pilgrims to St. James along the Camino.[1] Santo Domingo de la Calzada is famous among pilgrims for being the town of the "hanged innocent." The legend holds that a young man on pilgrimage with his family spurned the unchaste attentions of a local girl, who spitefully and cruelly planted a silver goblet in his traveling sack and accused him of theft. He was charged, found guilty, and hung. On their return from Santiago de Compostela his family found

1. Gitlitz and Davidson, *Pilgrimage Road to Santiago,* 154–55.

him still hanging on the scaffold but very much alive, sustained through the intercession of St. James. His parents pled with the magistrate for his release, who responded with incredulity, claiming that the boy was as dead as the roast chicken on his dinnerplate—at which point the chickens were divinely resurrected and begin to crow. And to this day two live chickens live in a coop in the nave of the cathedral. This story is not unique to Santo Domingo de la Calzada. It is part of the national identity of neighboring Portugal as the "Cock of Barcelos" and also exists in versions in Cologne and Toulouse, among other places.[2]

We experienced a fascinating thing as we walked out of Santo Domingo. There is a small roadside chapel (Ermita del Puente) near the bridge the saint constructed over the Rio Oja. As we approached, the church bell started ringing lustily and continuously. Fireworks exploded overhead. Many people wearing the red scarves of the *Cofradía* gathered around the chapel. An elderly Spanish couple was walking next to us— obviously locals. I asked what all the excitement was about and she went on at length about something or other. I picked up three words: Mass, chapel, and bridge. From this I gathered that on this day every year the citizens of the town celebrate something having to do with the bridge. A very special day indeed. Yes, I'm sure that's what she told me. Definitely. As it turns out, the atmospherics at the bridge's chapel is just one event in a much longer series of celebratory activities that honor the saint every year between May 10 and May 15. We were disappointed to have missed the other festivities, which include:

- ⁖ Sharing of the "Saint's Bread" by the town's young ladies adorned in traditional costume
- ⁖ The decorating and parading of the *Carneros del Santo* (Saint's rams)
- ⁖ Installment of the new Prior and Prioress
- ⁖ The free lunch for residents and pilgrims consisting of 225 kg of mutton, eighty kg of chickpeas, eighty kg of chard, ten kg of leek, and three kg of beacon, onions, parsley, and other ingredients. It is shared out with sixty large loaves of bread, washed down by one hundred liters of wine.[3]

2. Orlin, "Case for Anecdotalism," 52–77.

3. See https://www.alberguecofradiadelsanto.com/en/traditions-and-ceremonies/

As we walked through the countryside after passing through Santo Domingo de la Calzada we ran into a couple who were toting their backpacks on a pull-behind golf cart. After running into the fellow from the day before who was strolling The Way with nothing but a lone golf club, I began to wonder what we might see next? Tiger Woods teeing off in Terradillos de los Templarios? Tom Watson putting for a birdie in Triacastela? Well, I was not prepared to rule anything out. But I tip my hat to this guy's ingenuity in lightening his load through this method.

I was bitterly disappointed to miss the free lunch in Santo Domingo de la Calzada. The only thing better than lunch is a free lunch. We assuaged our misfortune with a stop in Grañon. We spotted some smoked oysters on the grocer's shelf—a delicious new filling for our sandwiches.

We arrived around noon at our destination—Viloria de la Rioja. The Albergue Parada Viloria was a very old building with leaning walls, crooked stairs, and bracingly cold showers. The *hospitaleros*—Toni and Mariaje— were gracious hosts who prepared a delightful paella for our shared evening meal. Staying in the *albergue* with us that night were Katje and Rainbow, along with John and Joan from South Carolina. There was also an Estonian couple and our friend Tasmania Pris. Joan was a bit hyper. When not hyper, she was worried. I am sure she was a lovely person but her general state of anxiety was something I had to try to ignore. Perhaps she was an angel sent to teach me patience.

The leaky skies of the morning gave way to bright sunshine as we lazed about killing time during the afternoon. There was a bench in a small plaza across the street where Craig and I lounged—hobo style—as we observed the comings and goings of pilgrims with loftier goals for the day.

While I'm guessing that most days in Viloria de la Rioja (which is, improbably, located in Castilla y León—not La Rioja) are real yawners, we were in luck. In an equally surprising bit of Spanish place name confoundery, it turns out that St. Dominic of the Highway was not born in the town to the east that bears his name, but in Viloria de la Rioja. And we were there on the day that the town's forty citizens were celebrating. City Hall was festooned with colorful banners commemorating his birthday in 1019. Toni and Mariaje called us all to supper and then beat feet to join their thirty-eight neighbors in a tent up the street where much drinking, singing, and banqueting was in progress.

And as it turns out, Viloria de la Rioja is a plucky little village filled with rural activists. The citizens were understandably concerned that the town could fold if the Camino was not supported to continue running through the village's lone street. There was talk of relocating the path to run parallel to the nearby A-12 highway as part of a road improvement project. This has led to protests, marches, letter-writing campaigns, and all manner of redress for this understandable grievance. I hope the good people of that place are successful in convincing the powers-that-be of the justice of their claim, for no pilgrim prefers walking next to a busy highway when s/he could be strolling through a village, even one as moribund as this one.

"Viloria de Rioja is on the Camino" (and not next to the highway).

Chapter 12

Viloria de la Rioja to Villafranca Montes de Oca

O Lord my God, make me poor without discouragement.
— *Aquinas, Aquinas Prayer Book*

I AWOKE from a good night's sleep, though it was very chilly. When we left the *albergue* the temperature was a mere 37° F, which made for brisk walking under what would evolve into bright blue skies once the sun finally rose.

Sometimes we awoke to the alarm on my phone. Sometimes we awoke to the natural urgings of our aging bodies. Sometimes we awoke for reasons that were not altogether clear. And sometimes we awoke because our fellow pilgrims were just loud enough to disturb our slumber. We have been guilty of such behavior, so I do not wish to shut the door on reconciliation with these whispering bag-rustlers. It was Anxious Joan who jarred us from sweet dreams in the Viloria *albergue*. I first became aware of her movements as one in the fog of a dream. Dim scratchings on distant surfaces. Sounds I could not identify. As conscious awareness gradually replaced the lacy mists of slumber I became attuned to the fact that something, somewhere was moving about, and noisily.

No problem, my mind encouraged. *Just ignore it and go back to sleep. You have a hard day of walking ahead of you. You need your rest.*

This seemed like excellent advice. But it turns out that my mind was a weak match for the gratings of plastic grocery bags being filled, emptied, and refilled afresh. This was not a loud sound necessarily, but it had an outsized effect—much like a small pebble trapped in one's shoe. After a few minutes I turned from the wall, opened one eye, and spied Anxious Joan's hands worrying over her possessions like an occultist divining the future over a table of animal bones. "Darn it" was not the expression that came to mind as I realized that the evening had come to an end and a new day had arrived—even if prematurely. I stumbled from the lower bunk, grumbled Craig awake, headed out into the star-filled morning darkness, and started walking west. Goodbye Anxious Joan and your bedevilling, worrisome plastic bags.

As we walked between Viloria de la Rioja to Villafranca Montes de Oca I was cognizant that I was missing Mother's Day back home. I missed the moms in my life, and not a little bit. I hoped they were all OK, and I looked forward to the day when I would see them again.

The first village we came to after leaving Viloria de la Rioja was Villa-mayor del Rio. It was closed for business on that chilly morning. It may, in fact, be closed for business every morning. And perhaps in the afternoons and evenings too. A brief TripAdvisor search of things to do in Villamayor del Rio returns a blank page. Belorado—and breakfast—was only four kilo-meters farther.

We found that our coffee stop in Belorado was insufficient to satisfy, so we made a second stop in Villambistia. There we ran into Anne from Ireland, whom we had seen from time to time along the way. She was having her pack forwarded and staying in private accommodations, having booked in advance with a tour company. She was a delightful person and a diverting conversationalist during our coffee break.

Craig's son-in-law works for a company that manufactures automatic openers for garage doors and similar applications. It is interesting how layered and nuanced such a seemingly mundane appliance can be. Craig fascinated me with long soliloquies on the problems to be overcome in opening doors in an automated fashion, elegies to new developments now available to an expanding marketplace, and sonnets devoted to entering and exiting buildings with encumbered hands and arms. Each new town presented fresh examples for how Spain is overcoming the problems associated with manual egress and ingress.

**Belorado's lovely
Plaza Mayor awash in morning light.**

We'd been walking for eleven days without a break by this point in our pilgrimage. Our legs were feeling the miles. My feet were sending me messages suggesting the various benefits of a day off. We were planning on a rest day in Burgos, but that was still more than fifty kilometers away. Though we only walked twenty kilometers on the way to Villafranca Montes de Oca, and despite the fact that we felt like we could have gone farther, we decided that this village at the foot of the Oca Hills was a good place to end the day. Unless we walked an additional sixteen difficult kilometers beyond Villafranca, we wouldn't get to Burgos any sooner, so we opted for an easier pace.

The *albergue* in Villafranca Montes de Oca was the one at which Joe and I stayed in 2016. It was very nice, which is surprising since it is 650 years old. The Hotel San Antón Abad was built by the Queen of Castile Doña Juana Manuel, wife of King Enrique II, to service *peregrinos* who passed through Villafranca Montes de Oca on their way to the shrine of St. James. Fortunately for Craig and me, the place had been completely renovated in a comfortable, modern style and now offers a lovely restaurant in addition to the usual pilgrim amenities. For fourteenth-century pilgrims it offered a crust of bread, a cup of watered wine, and a place to die and be buried with dignity.[1] Modernity has its advantages.

The walk between Viloria de la Rioja to Villafranca Montes de Oca was shared by lots of pilgrims we had met earlier in our pilgrimage, including Katje (Germany), George (Hungary), Klaus (Germany), Lu (Japan), and Mags (Australia). We also ran into Laura from the Netherlands, who should not be confused with Laura from Switzerland or Laura from Denmark. We had the good fortune to meet Ann and Carl from Sweden as we climbed the last hill before entering Villafranca. Ann had just retired from a career in healthcare a couple of weeks previously. The Camino was her first big adventure in the retired state of life. She and Carl were lovely people with whom we would have many conversations throughout the remainder of the walk to Santiago de Compostela.

I went to Mass in the village church with about fifty of the local inhabitants—each of which put the "senior" in senior citizen. I had a nice chat with an eightysomething gentleman on the church porch before Mass began. I think he understood everything I said. I understood perhaps 25 percent of what he said. All in all I'd call it a success. He related his sadness at how towns such as his have emptied of young families in recent years. This is a significant problem for most rural Spanish towns and villages.

Craig and I enjoyed a very unpilgrim-like dinner in the *albergue's* restaurant that evening. Craig had garlic soup and mackerel. I had potato and chorizo soup with beef stew. Tiramisu for both of us for dessert. The next day we had a very hilly seventeen-mile walk through the Montes de Oca as we made our way toward Burgos and twenty-four hours of pampered civilization. We needed this sustaining meal to fuel our journey. I can hear you judging us. Stop it.

After dinner we chatted with fellow pilgrims, collected laundry from the line in the side yard, and made our preparations for bed. Regrettably,

---

1. A medieval pilgrimage really was a dangerous, life-threatening undertaking. One of the major pilgrim hospitals in Pamplona described the pilgrims encountered during a typical week: "3 sick poor people from Flanders . . . A beggar from Montalban with 3 wounds; coming back from Santiago he stayed 3 days . . . 4 very sick poor people on their way back from Santiago, 3 from Bordeaux and 1 a Flemming, and 3 of them were nearly dead, so much so that the Flemming stayed 12 days . . . The day of Our Lady of September a poor man from Toulouse coming back from Santiago fell ill here and 9 days later he died . . ." (Frauca, "De Pamplona a Puente La Reina," 12–13).

the *hospitalero* assigned two Italian young lovers to the top bunks above Craig and me. They were chatty youths. In fact, They. Just. Would. Not. Be. Quiet. Blahbity blahbity blah in rapid-fire loud Italian. As I pushed my earplugs a bit deeper into my skull I hoped I'd snore like a freighter just to get even. Another sin to confess . . .

Chapter 13

Villafranca Montes de Oca to Cardeñuela de Riopico

The best way to show my gratitude is to accept everything, even my problems, with joy.

—St. Teresa of Calcutta[1]

W HEN one walks in the dark it is comforting to have a headlamp to light the way, illuminate the ankle-twisting rocks, and find the waymarks. My headlamp quit on me five minutes into the morning's hike up into the Forest of Oca under an inky sky with brilliant stars overhead. Craig lit the way for the two of us.

The hike through the Montes de Oca was steep, lonely, and beautiful. (HJ.Weinz, CC BY-SA 3.0, via Wikimedia Commons)

1 Fakes, G.R.A.C.E., 14.

The Oca forest has a history from medieval times of banditry, witch-craft, and all manner of gloomy reputation. Indeed, forested places have long been avoided by clear-thinking people throughout the ages. Medievals thought of them as haunted, enchanted, thin places populated by dragons, dwarfs, elves, fairies, giants, gnomes, goblins, imps, ogres, trolls, unicorns, and other mythical creatures of ill intent.[2] Perhaps that is why none of the folks that used to live in the Oca forest stuck around for long, the area changing hands from Astur, Cantabri, Visigoth, Basque, and Moor before finally settling firmly in the Castillian kingdom. Much of the day's first twelve kilometers were through these woods. There were steep ascents and descents, with a long, flat section at the mountaintop. The dark legends about the place must have discouraged any permanent population. We ran into nobody except for a few pilgrims.[3]

The haunted forest shrouded in gloom. (Peter Balcerzak,
CC BY-SA 3.0, via Wikimedia Commons)

Roughly halfway through the spooky forest we came to a very sobering place. El Monumento de los Caídos (Monument to the Fallen) commemo-rates the mass burial of 300 partisans from the Burgos area murdered during the Spanish Civil War. As we read the inscription on the stone obelisk while

2. Briggs, *Encyclopedia of Fairies*, 227.

3. Pilgrims to Santiago de Compostela have been losing their way in the forests of the Montes de Oca for centuries. David Gitliz and Linda Kay Davidson report being lost in this forest as recently as 1974 (Gitliz and Davidson, *Pilgrimage Road to Santiago*, 166).

the darkened sky began to brighten in the east, it seemed to me that the war was perhaps too easy for pilgrims to ignore, forget, or otherwise remain in ignorance about. Coming face to face with a mass grave in a modern European nation helped me understand that peace and security are illusory concepts, easily replaced by fanaticism, partisanship, and unbridled, naked power.

Civil war and its aftermath. (KRLS, CC BY-SA 4.0, via Wikimedia Commons)

Craig carried with him a packet of dated letters from his daughter. This was a touching gesture on her part, and was a powerfully emotive way to help keep her Dear Old Dad connected to those he loved back home. The letter for that day suggested that—as one way to keep our spirits up— we recount our favorite films to each other. We thought this was a grand idea. I have three memories of those miles. First, while I cannot remember Craig's list of favorite films, I do recall that he has seen just about every movie ever made. His knowledge and experience in this field of human endeavor was seemingly limitless. My second memory is that the game was entirely diverting. The miles simply melted away as "Name Your Favorite Movie" evolved into "Name Your Favorite Song" before we moved on to

"Name Your Favorite Book." Finally, I remember listing my top films: *It's a Wonderful Life, Forrest Gump,* and *The Wizard of Oz.* Though on second thought, *A Christmas Carol* is also a wonderful movie. The old, black-and-white version. Also, *Saving Private Ryan* made quite an impression on me. Hmmm . . . *The Lord of the Rings* trilogy seems worthy of my admiration. Pilgriming, it seems, is not all prayers and devotions all the time.

Our first coffee break was in San Juan de Ortega. St. John of the Nettles is another example of some Spanish villages' utter disregard for place names designed to attract visitors and permanent residents. This did not deter the until-then childless Queen Isabella[4] from coming to pray at the shrine of San Juan, who is the patron saint of both innkeepers and infertility. Two children later, the queen wasn't about to let a few nettles keep her down.

Isabella "the Catholic." (Luis de Madrazo, Public domain, via Wikimedia Commons)

The coffee shop sat across the lone street from the only other thing in that town—an ancient monastery. Lu from Japan joined us. An hour later as we passed through Agés we thought it prudent to get a second cup. This

---

4. Queen Isabella deserves more attention in this account than space allows. Best remembered for financing Columbus's voyage to the New World, she also (1) united Spain as a single nation, (2) booted Muslims and Jews from the country, (3) launched the Inquisition, and (4) was the first named woman to appear on both a US stamp and a US coin. She was very devout, and named both her children—Juan and Juana—after the saint she credited for divine intercession in being able to conceive.

time we coupled it with toast with margarine and homemade marmalade. I spoke with the lady of the establishment—a delightful woman—in Spanish and understood 20 percent of what she said with perfect clarity.

We transited through Atapuerca—a UNESCO site[5] containing the earliest human ancestors in Europe—and began the long climb up to the Matagrande Plain with its view of Burgos in the distance. The Spanish army was practicing cannonading in the military reserve to our left.

We pulled into the *albergue* in Cardeñuela de Riopico around noon after a walk of nearly seventeen miles. Burgos was tempting, but we did not think we had eight miles left in our feet. We were the first ones to arrive at the *albergue*, which was typical since we often began our day's walk earlier than most pilgrims. Others in our pilgrim bubble began to roll in over the next two hours. Katje, Rainbow, Lu, Tyghe the Dutch kid, and Ann and Carl were among those with whom we shared the *albergue* that evening. While doing my laundry I spied the chatty Italian lovers from the previous night arrive. Thankfully, the *hospitalero* assigned them beds in another bunkroom. God bless him.

It was a chilly day, but the sun was shining brightly and provided a warming environment in which to lounge the afternoon away. I spoke at length with a Danish medical student named Laura (not to be confused with Swiss medical student Laura, or Dutch Laura, who comes from the same town as Craig's wife's parents). She was desperately trying to discern if she should continue in medicine or switch her program, which would require her to start university all over again. She felt really stuck. I hoped she could find some peace of mind about this on her pilgrimage. Her vocational dilemma caused me to reflect on the relative merits of the US higher education system that encourages a program of general education before pursuing professional training. There are some US students who would do very well in the European system, which is based in theory on the Humboldtian model[6] with its roots in nineteenth-century Germany. Unfortunately, Wilhelm von Humboldt's concept of education has morphed in most European universities into an education-as-labor market-preparation training program. Regrettably, universities in the United States are beginning to follow suit. Many are already fully transitioned. This system is more likely to produce excellent technocrats for occupations that technology is

5. United Nations Educational, Scientific, and Cultural Organization, "Archaeological Site of Atapuerca."

6. Josephson et al., *Humboldtian Tradition*, 143.

rapidly rendering obsolete, but less likely to produce virtuous citizens well prepared for jobs that have not yet been imagined. The American humorist Garrison Keillor parodies the situation in this way:

> America is the land of second and third chances, not like Europe. We have remedial colleges for kids who slept through high school. In Europe, the system is geared toward efficiency: it separates kids by age 12 into Advanced, Mediocre, and Food Service Workers, and once they assign you to a lane, it's hard to get out of it. In this country, if our children are lazy and undisciplined, we try to see signs of artistic ability. We put them in a fine arts program. They spend three years writing weird stuff and get an MFA and you drive through McDonald's and the young people fixing the Egg McMuffins are poets and songwriters.[7]

Remember, Dear Reader, it's a parody. Educational systems notwithstanding, I hoped for the best for Laura. She was a lovely person.

There was no store in that metropolis of 111 people, so the luncheon menu featured the dribs and drabs left in our backpacks from the previous day's grocery shopping. We participated in the shared pilgrim meal later that evening in the *albergue*. The meal was great, with large platters of salad, a couple of stewed chicken drumsticks, a bowl of delicious soup, fries, a smoothie palate cleanser, and pudding for dessert. It was fun sharing experiences with those seated near us. Lots of *communitas*.

As the sky darkened and we prepared to end another day, I took another look at the notes I had been receiving from home. The photos of the grandkiddos warmed my heart, filled me with gratitude for the many blessings in my life, and allowed me to drift off to sleep with a smile.

7. Keillor, "Art of Love," 2.

Chapter 14

Cardeñuela de Riopico
to Burgos

O Lord my God, make me chaste without regret.
— Aquinas, Aquinas Prayer Book

CRAIG and I took our time getting out of bed and packing up in Cardeñuela since we had a relatively short walk that day. We did not even set an alarm for the morning. Only eight miles to Burgos and a day of rest and relaxation. The heck with the alarm.

There are three routes to enter Burgos. The most pleasant—the one Joe and I walked in 2016—is not well-marked but runs alongside the river through a long park. If one keeps the river on the right one cannot help but eventually run into downtown Burgos. If, on the other hand, one falls into friendly, engaging conversation with Klaus from Bavaria, well, I'm not sure what happened, but Craig and I missed the turn for the pleasant river route and ended up on the path that runs through the industrial outskirts instead. What should have been an easy three-hour amble through a verdant arbor bordered by a babbling waterway turned into a walk next to a four-lane road filled with whizzing traffic as we passed by factory after factory that manufactured the various necessities of modern Spanish life.

The road less traveled to Burgos. (Muso006, CC BY-SA 3.0, via Wikimedia Commons)

There were two redeeming aspects of our map-reading *faux pas*. The first involved my conversation with Klaus. He was a delightful chap on a month-long leave of absence from his job at a company that makes small motors for a variety of applications. He lived in or near the Black Forest, and his tales of weekend hikes in that famous place effectively diverted my attention from the gritty outskirts of East Burgos. The second enjoyable aspect of our unchosen route presented itself when we stopped for a coffee in Villafria. There we met Elizabeth—Liz to us pilgrims—from Capetown. She appeared to be walking by herself. She was looking for a way to take a bus into the old town center of Burgos and avoid the industrial section that awaited Craig and me. There was a bus stop outside the coffee shop, but she could not speak Spanish to make inquiries with the bartender to find out when the bus would arrive. Gringo Rich to the rescue. A few phrases of flawless Spanish later and Craig and I waved goodbye to Liz as she rode in publicly accommodated comfort past the factories. We hoisted our packs and trudged west.

We arrived at Hotel Norte y Londres around 11:00 after picking up some groceries for lunch on the way into the city center. A well-meaning local tried to direct us to the Camino path even though we wanted to go to the hotel. Eventually we talked him into giving us directions to the place we wished to go instead of the place he desired for us, and all was *muchas gracias* and *muchisimas gracias*.

After showering, laundry, and a stern lecture to the day's newest blister we brought our lunch fixins to the cathedral square and took in its awesome grandeur while we munched our sandwiches. There were little kids wearing school uniforms and blue caps holding hands as their parents or preschool teachers paraded them through the square. This touching scene caused me to miss the tykes in my life afresh.

Burgos Cathedral, one of Spain's most amazing churches.
(Luis Rogelio HM, CC BY-SA 2.0, via Wikimedia Commons)

We toured the cathedral, which is simply one of the most amazing places I have been. Here's what UNESCO has to say about the place:

> Construction on the Cathedral began in 1221 and was completed in 1567. It is a comprehensive example of the evolution of Gothic style, with the entire history of Gothic art exhibited in its superb architecture and unique collection of art, including paintings, choir stalls, reredos, tombs, and stained-glass windows.
>
> The plan of the Cathedral is based on a Latin Cross of harmonious proportions of 84 by 59 metres. The three-story elevation, the vaulting, and the tracery of the windows are closely related to contemporary models of the north of France. The portals of the transept (the *Puerta del Sarmental* to the south and the *Puerta de la Coronería* to the north) may also be compared to the great sculpted ensembles of the French royal domain, while the enamelled, brass tomb of Bishop Mauricio resembles the so-called

Limoges goldsmith work. Undertaken after the Cathedral, the two-storied cloister, which was completed towards 1280, still fits within the framework of the French high Gothic.

After a hiatus of nearly 200 years, work resumed on the Burgos Cathedral towards the middle of the 15th century and continued for more than 100 years. The work done during this time consisted of embellishments of great splendour, assuring the Cathedral's continued world-renown status. The workshop was composed of an international team, and among the most famous architects were Juan de Colonia, soon relieved by his son Simon (responsible for the towers and open spires of the facade, the Constable's chapel, and the Saint Anne's chapel) and Felipe de Borgoña, assisted by numerous collaborators (responsible for the choir, cupola, and lantern tower over the transept crossing). When two of these architects, Juan de Vallejo and Juan de Castañeda, completed the prodigious cupola with its starred vaulting in 1567, the Burgos Cathedral unified one of the greatest known concentrations of late Gothic masterpieces: the *Puerta de la Pellejería* (1516) of Francisco de Colonia, the ornamental grill and choir stalls, the grill of the chapel of the Presentation (1519), the retable of Gil de Siloe in the Constable's chapel, the retable of Gil de Siloe and Diego de la Cruz in Saint Anne's chapel, the staircase of Diego de Siloe in the north transept arm (1519), the tombs of Bishop Alonso de Cartagena, Bishop Alonso Luis Osorio de Acuña, the Abbot Juan Ortega de Velasco, the Constable Pedro Hernández de Velasco and, his wife Doña Mencía de Mendoza, etc.[1]

It was nap time after our exhausting, energy-sapping tour of the cathedral. We were supposed to be resting after all. There you go again with the judgment.

I went to Mass in the cathedral's Chapel of the Santísimo Cristo de Burgos at 7:30 and met Craig afterward in the square. We had enjoyed a bit of a happy hour before Mass so we didn't feel like dinner. We stopped at a lovely cafe on the esplanade near the river. Craig had a beer and I had some ice cream. It was fun watching the Burgosians (Burgosites?) in their hundreds and thousands taking in the cool spring evening.

I wrote my notes for this chapter in the main square of the city as the moon hung overhead and the streetlights began to flicker to life. People were still very much out and about. I had been praying for a long list of

1. United Nations Educational, Scientific, and Cultural Organization. "Burgos Cathedral." 2-4.

people on this pilgrimage, and hoped that each would receive what he or she needed. The plaza was a wonderful place to lean back, relax, and recall each of these people to my mind, commending each to God and His infinite mercy. Each is very dear to me. Very dear indeed.

We thoroughly enjoyed a restful day off in Burgos after sleeping in until 7:30. We had purchased groceries for a hotel room breakfast the previous day. It seemed to us altogether civilized to throw off the pilgrim-y habits of the past two weeks by lounging in underclothes with feet liberated from the tyranny of hiking shoes. We nibbled our continental breakfast while observing the city's denizens slowly throw off the lethargy of the previous night's slumber as they made their way to work and school through Plaza Alonso-Martínez two stories below our large bay window. Could any King of Castile claim a grander perch, a more lavish meal, or a more decadent beginning to the day? We thought not.

Though our grocery store breakfast was wonderful, we lacked the ability to brew coffee in our hotel room. This, we decided, must be remedied without delay. Freshly scrubbed, shaved, and shod we strolled through the city's streets, still damp from their early morning washing. It did not take long to find a coffee shop, our noses now trained like finely tuned caffeine-sensing divining rods.

What do two road-weary pilgrims do with twenty-four hours at-large? We had heard good things about the Museum of Human Evolution,[2] which houses artifacts from the nearby Atapuerca archeological site. It was not far from the hotel, so we strolled past the monumental statue of El Cid Campeador,[3] over the Rio Arlanzón, and up to the grand plaza that serves as the museum's front door. We approached the pleasant young woman at the ticket counter. We held our pilgrim *credencials* prominently in our hands, hoping our status as holy, sanctified wanderers might gain us admission at a reduced fee. The agent smiled sweetly, looked us up and down, and determined that we were pilgrims without needing written proof. I am

2. https://www.museoevolucionhumana.com/en/the-museum.

3. Rodrigo Díaz de Vivar (c.1043–10 July 1099) was a Castilian knight and warlord in medieval Spain. The Moors called him El Cid, which meant the Lord (probably from the original Arabic *al-sayyid*), and the Christians, El Campeador, which stood for "The Battlefielder," "Outstanding Warrior," or "The one who stands out in the battlefield." He was born in Vivar del Cid, a town near the city of Burgos. After his death, he became Spain's celebrated national hero and the protagonist of the most significant medieval Spanish epic poem, *El Cantar de Mio Cid*. To this day, El Cid remains a popular Spanish folk-hero and national icon, with his life and deeds remembered in plays, films, folktales, songs, and video games. (Fletcher, *Quest for El Cid*, 166–68, 198).

not sure how she figured this out. I suppose she must have received special training for such occasions. She asked our ages, and informed us that the elderly may pass without cost. Well. The museum was excellent, with all the displays in both Spanish and English. As accomplished as I am in the Spanish language, I read the English displays to avoid the sin of pride.

Museum-going is fatiguing, hungry work. Back to the hotel for a sandwich and Nap #1.

Suitably refueled and refreshed we decided that a late-afternoon tour of the castle that sits on the heights overlooking the city would be a diverting way to pass the time. We had the place practically to ourselves. The views of the cathedral spires—surrounded by both the old and newer sections of the town, framed by the greater expanse of the Arlanzón Valley—was rather breathtaking. As we scrambled around the mostly derelict walls of the historic fortification we ran into a family from Pittsburgh whose son was marrying a Spanish woman in Logroño in a few days. It's always comforting when traveling abroad to encounter people from one's home country, trade impressions of the trip, and pass along tidbits of experience offered in a spirit of patriotic fraternity. Still, reflecting on the international nature of that young man's impending nuptials made me grateful that all my kin live close to me. Very grateful indeed.

Climbing up to the castle was warm work, so a beer under a shady awning in the main plaza was both deserved and enjoyed. I went to Mass in the cathedral again, and Craig met me afterward for dinner. He was suffering from Acute Hamburger Deficiency Syndrome and had therefore conducted research sufficient to locate the most authentically Spanish restaurant in the city that could ease the pangs of this dreaded touristic malady—"The Good Burger." Had the proprietors offered us a comment card I might have suggested changing the name of the establishment to "The Just OK Burger."

While taking a day off from pilgriming was pleasantly diverting and corporally rejuvenating, our minds began to lean into the next day, and to the next stage of our journey. We decided to set the alarm for 5:00 am so we could get an early start on the next day's twenty-mile walk. After we left Burgos we would enter the *meseta*, and would have long views and no shade for the next week at least. Even though I had walked the *meseta* before, I'll confess to a feeling of anticipatory anxiety about this stage of the pilgrimage. I am not sure what caused this. Perhaps I just missed Carol.

A phone call home before going to sleep helped and put me in mind of
Edith Wharton's musings:

> Let us be lovers to the end,
> O you to whom my soul is given,
> Whose smiles have turned this earth to heaven,
> Fast holding hands as we descend
> Life's pathway devious and uneven,
> Let us be lovers to the end.
> Dear, let us make of Time a friend
> To bind us closer with his cares,
> And though grief strike us unawares
> No poisoned shaft that fate can send
> Shall wound us through each other's prayers,
> If we are lovers to the end.
> Let us be lovers to the end
> And, growing blind as we grow old,
> Refuse forever to behold
> How age has made the shoulders bend
> And Winter blanched the hair's young gold.
> Let us be lovers to the end.
> Whichever way our footsteps tend
> Be sure that, if we walk together,
> They'll lead to realms of sunny weather,
> By shores where quiet waters wend.
> At eventide we shall go thither,
> If we are lovers to the end.[4]

4. Wharton and Goldman-Price, *Selected Poems*, 117.

Chapter 15

Burgos to Hontanas

O Lord my God, make me patient without complaint.
— Aquinas, Aquinas Prayer Book

T HE Camino Frances can be thought of as existing in three sections. St. Jean Pied-de-Port to Burgos is the first third. It is filled with rolling hills interspersed with mini-mountains. It is beautiful, but physically challenging. It has a varied and interesting history, and its towns, villages, and cities have their own distinctive character. The second third of the Camino is the one we entered as we left Burgos—the *meseta central*. It is a huge upland plain that occupies a significant portion of Spain's interior. Spanning the Camino from Burgos to just beyond León, it has an average elevation of roughly 3,000 feet above sea level. The pilgrim is challenged in this section with long distances, direct sun exposure, and monotonous landscapes. It is not without its charms (it is positively alive with birds—including the eagle we saw just before Hontanas, for example), but the miles generate plenty of opportunity for prayer, introspection, and other internal dialogues. The last third of the walk—which for us was still at least a week away—is mountainous, green, wet, and forested.

Long, lonely views on the *meseta*.

Knowing that the afternoon sun on the *meseta* can be uncomfortable, we awoke in our Burgos hotel at 5:00 a.m. and snuck away from the city under cover of darkness. We were already west of the city's suburbs when the sun rose, revealing pink clouds and the promise of a good day for walking.

We encountered a few hills that day where the Camino descends to valleys containing creeks and rivers, but the walking was generally flat. We arrived at our destination in Hontanas at 12:30. This town has the distinction of being invisible until you arrive at its very edge since it sits in a valley.

Pilgrims seeking shelter and refreshment in Hontanas.
(Kolossus, CC BY-SA 3.0, via Wikimedia Commons)

The *albergue* we checked into is the same one Joe and I stayed in in 2016, though I think it has a new owner. We shared a room with a Dutchman, Fred, who was travelling the Camino by bike. He seemed nice enough, though he had a bit of a droopy face. Bits of his lunch seemed to cling to his lips. One wanted to toss him a napkin. I found myself staring at a spot in the middle of his forehead when speaking with him to avoid being distracted by the bits of sandwich which did not quite make it all the way into his pie-hole. That said, he was an interesting conversation partner, as was Harold—our other roommate—who was from the Indian Ocean island nation of Mauritius. Fascinating guy.

My body was holding up reasonably well. My knees were achy after the long walk, and I was still searching for the right system to knock back the blisters on my left foot. I bought some Vaseline at a pharmacy in Burgos and smeared my toes liberally before setting off for Hontanas. It seemed to help a bit.

We took two coffee breaks that morning—one in Tosantos while we watched a weather report on a Burgos TV station (rain that night, we thought), and the second in Hornillos Del Camino next to the town's public fountain. TV meteorologists in Spain are similar in many respects to their American counterparts: perky folks with wide grins, even in the face of an approaching hurricane—perhaps *especially* in the face of an approaching hurricane. Bad weather is their moment to shine, after all. "Good morning from WBAD! The weather today is going to be epically, civilization-extinguishingly, species-eliminatingly awful! Isn't that great!" In English or in Spanish, the worse the weather, the more joyous they are.

The church next door to the *albergue* advertised a Mass at 6:00. Craig and I attended, and the priest asked me to read from St. Paul's Epistle to the Corinthians: "Love is patient, love is kind . . ." After the Mass he called all the pilgrims to the front, presented us with a small silver cross, and blessed us. It was a moving experience.

We enjoyed a shared pilgrim meal in the *albergue*'s dining room with Harold. The food and the conversation were delightful. We would spend much of what remained of our pilgrimage with Harold. The wonderful conversations, shared faith experience, and Harold's all-around friendliness were good reminders of all I had to be grateful for.

Chapter 16

Hontanas to Boadilla del Camino

O Lord my God, make me humble without posturing.

—*Aquinas, Aquinas Prayer Book*

I T rained in the night, though how hard I wasn't sure. We were out on the path by 6:00 dodging muddy puddles in the slippery clay while a brilliant orange moon slowly dipped between clouds and eventually below the surrounding hills.

Walking by moonlight, surrounded by hills. (Photo by Kym MacKinnon on Unsplash)

Dawn brought clearing skies which would eventually turn cloudy. It was a chilly day—often with a stiff breeze, which forced me reluctantly into a jacket. Although not all agree,[1] St. Teresa of Ávila is alleged to have said "All weather is good weather for it is God's." We trudged on through the "good" weather.

About six kilometers after leaving Hontanas, we passed by the haunted ruins of the fifteenth-century convent of San Antón and made our way to Castrojeriz with its mountaintop castle. There we caught a lady opening her bar for the day. She made us fried eggs and bacon to enjoy with our first coffee of the day. Castrojeriz is wrapped around the side of a small mountain. Or was it a tall hill? When does a hill become a mountain? This is evidently a charged question. Google it and you will get 317 million hits. I imagine that conferences on the topic are marked by lively exchanges between various factions of geographers. Our guidebook calls the landmass a "steep mesa." This description is unhelpful since a mesa is a "flat-topped mountain or hill."[2] A mesa can evidently be a mountain or a hill. I have no idea what the pile of rock and soil around which Castrojeriz is wrapped actually is. Somebody ought to clarify things.

Castrojeriz and its derelict mountaintop/hilltop Castillo de San Esteban. (Gerd Eichmann, CC BY-SA 4.0, via Wikimedia Commons)

1. Fatherhorton, "St. Teresa of Ávila and the Weather."
2 Mesa, National Geographic, 1.

Thus fortified, we pushed on across the Tierra de Campos (Land of Fields) with its crisscrossing wheat fields sprinkled with bright red poppies. It was hard to avoid wondering if the fields of Flanders looked as peaceful 100 years ago:

> In Flanders fields the poppies blow
> Between the crosses, row on row,
>> That mark our place; and in the sky
>> The larks, still bravely singing, fly
> Scarce heard amid the guns below.
> We are the Dead. Short days ago
> We lived, felt dawn, saw sunset glow,
>> Loved and were loved, and now we lie,
>> In Flanders fields.
> Take up our quarrel with the foe:
> To you from failing hands we throw
>> The torch; be yours to hold it high.
>> If ye break faith with us who die
> We shall not sleep, though poppies grow
>> In Flanders fields.[3]

At Second Coffee in Itero de Vega we ran into Dutch Laura and the ever-present Mags. We picked up a few victuals for an eventual lunch and tucked these into our packs for the final six miles of our eighteen-mile walk. Our guidebook was precise in its instructions for how to navigate the complexities of Itero de Vega's decidedly unurban built environment: "Continue through town and leave via a wide dirt road." Well, at least the dirt road was wide.

There should not be a hill as high and steep as the Alto de Mostelares on the *meseta*. There just shouldn't be. But there it was. Any height of land called the "Mule Killing Incline" placed in a land as flat as the Tierra de Campos must be God's idea of how to test a pilgrim's resolve. I wonder how many people have climbed halfway up and chucked it all.

The sight of the church on the horizon indicating the promise of our beds in Boadilla Del Camino was most welcome, as the blister on my little toe was darkening my thoughts. The *albergue* is the same one Joe and I stayed in during our 2016 Camino. It had a lovely garden and did a brisk business. It had a kind of chaotic busyness to it. We decided to forego clothes washing since the gloomy skies finally gave way to a gentle drizzle. Well, it

---

3. Wolff, *In Flanders Fields*, 1979.

was not so hot that day, so I'm sure I didn't perspire much. And pilgrims are merely a species of hobo, so a bit of body "bouquet" is not unexpected.

We met some interesting people during the day's walk. Enrico was a young man from Venice. He walked very fast, and for good reason. He had been walking for two months, having stepped out of his front door in March and thus begun his Camino from that point. Impressive.

We met Araceli in the *albergue* common room where she was nibbling a lunch of crackers and orange slices. She was born in Mexico but lives in California. She just finished physical therapy school and was treating herself with a Burgos-to-Santiago walking holiday before settling down to a new job. We would spend quite a bit of time walking with Araceli as we made our way to Santiago de Compostela. She was a delightful young lady.

An older German couple came in while we were eating our lunch. Peter positively stumbled to a chair and very nearly did not make it. Clearly exhausted, Erika spoke to him in soothing tones while he tried to drink some water and recover himself. We cut one of our apples in half and offered it to him. He accepted it gratefully, and a few minutes later we slipped an orange to Erika so she could further supplement his blood glucose. Peter should not have been on the Camino in my amateur opinion. Yet when I spoke to him later (with the help of Google Translate) he told me that this was his seventh Camino. Perhaps six would have been enough. They were in the bunks next to mine that night. I hoped he would feel better after a good night's sleep.

The next day would be the first time we would look for a bed without reservations. We were hoping to stay in the *albergue* run by the Santa Maria sisters, and they did not take reservations. We planned on an early start and hoped for the best.

We met John and Mandy from Australia at dinner and had a wonderful conversation. We traded emails and promised to stay in touch. They were just two more reasons for the deep sense of gratitude I felt as I drifted off to sleep in that tiny village of 166 souls.

Chapter 17

===========

Boadilla del Camino to Carrión de los Condes

O Lord my God, make me cheerful without frivolity.

—*Aquinas, Aquinas Prayer Book*

T HE walking in that part of Spain was physically easier than in the first third of the Camino, but the distances tended to be lengthier, with longer stretches between towns. It was lonelier somehow. Lots of pilgrims skip the *meseta*, but I cannot really understand why. There was a lot of natural beauty out there. And I have never walked anywhere that has more power to help me *think* than the *meseta*. Sages through the ages have gone to the mountains for enlightenment. Perhaps they should have gone to the *meseta*.

The walk was long, flat, and without much in the way of notable features. The lone exception was the series of locks along the Canal de Castilla in Frómista. This canal brings much needed water from the Cantabrian Mountains to irrigate the cereal-growing Tierra de Campos. As we walked past the locks, we commented on how interesting they were. And that was the last comment we made on anything until day's end. Still, I was grateful for this day out on the plains.

An office-seeker wishes us a *buen camino*.

We did not have reservations in Carrión de los Condes, but we arrived early enough to get a spot at the famous *albergue* operated by the Augustinian sisters in the back of the Santa Maria church. This is a very popular spot, and we had to line up to be admitted.

At 5:30, the sisters led a sing-along with the *peregrinos*. Pilgrims were invited to share their names, ages, country of residence, and motivations for their pilgrimage. There were some very powerful stories. A twenty-nine-year-old German—Anya—left everyone misty-eyed when she conveyed that her father recently died following a quarrel with her. She hadn't had a chance to make up with him before his death. Several others shared equally moving testimonies. It was a privilege to share in these stories.

The sisters of Santa Maria welcomed us with song and story.

Mass in the church followed the sing-along. The priest called the pilgrims forward for a special blessing, and the sisters gave each person a paper star to "light their way to Santiago." It really was quite nice.

We enjoyed a chat with Ira (pronounced "ear-ah") from Finland. She was walking alone and seemed a bit vulnerable that day. Her foot was hurting, and both Craig and I hoped that she would be OK. We had little to worry about. As our pilgrimage continued we would learn that Ira's sweet, friendly personality would endear her to pilgrims all the way to Santiago de Compostela. She remains a valued friend to this day.

Craig and Ira get to know each other while waiting to be admitted to Albergue Santa Maria del Camino.

We enjoyed a pre-Mass snack of chocolate, cheese, and tea with Mags, Rainbow, Lu, and Dutch Laura. Later, we went to a bar for dinner. Craig was chilly and asked if there was any soup available to warm him up. The server called back into the kitchen and was told there was one serving left. Craig thought himself lucky to get that last bowl of soup. That feeling would wear off soon.

Chapter 18

Carrión de los Condes to Terradillos de los Templarios

O Lord my God, make me mature without gloom.

— Aquinas, Aquinas Prayer Book

A s I typed the heading for this chapter it struck me that the smallest towns along the Camino often have the longest names. The 2,100 people of the two towns that anchored our walk that day require eight words and forty-three letters just to let folks know where they are. Calzadilla de la Cueza, through which we walked seventeen kilometers after beginning the day's walk, has fifty-four people, four words, and nineteen letters. Perhaps there was a village-naming contest in rural Spain at some point in the misty past. If so, the undisputed champion is the hamlet of Colinas del Campo de Martín Moro Toledano de Castilla y León, in the province of León. Its seventy-six residents require eleven words and fifty characters to describe their homeplace. Even this seeming fecundity of letters is no match for the longest place name in Europe. Llanfairpwllgwyngyllgogerychwyrndrobwll-llantysiliogogogoch—a Welsh village—is the king of European tongue-twisters at fifty-eight letters. Welsh speakers will recognize this place as

"Saint Mary's Church in a hollow of white hazel near the rapid whirlpool of the church of Saint Tysilio with a red cave"[1] Major cities like Burgos and León are more efficiently named.

By the time the train conductor announces this place the passengers may miss their stop. (Llanfairpwllgwyngyllgogerychwyrndrobwllllantysiliogogogoch by Steve Daniels, CC BY-SA 2.0, via Wikimedia Commons)

Wordiness in the naming of things is, of course, not restricted to hamlets and villages out in the middle of nowhere. In May 1817, the first private mental health hospital opened in the United States and was called the Asylum for the Relief of Persons Deprived of the Use of Their Reason.[2] A name clearly created by a committee—perhaps a committee composed of the hospital's patients.

Remember the warming remnant of soup that served as Craig's supper the previous evening? Well, it might have been a bit "off." Craig was ill three times in the night. His acute gastrointestinal distress was exacerbated by the fact that there was a pilgrim sleeping on a mattress in the hallway leading to the bathroom. Craig had quite a job of work trying not to throw up on the guy as he sprinted—in the dark—to the toilet. Still, he was up, dressed, and ready to walk by 6:00 a.m. We found a bar open as we crept out of town and purchased a can of iced tea for Craig to sip to keep him going. Was it food

1. Galloway, "UK's Longest Named Village," 4.
2. "Historical Events on May 15."

poisoning? According to the Mayo Clinic, victims of food poisoning may experience the following signs and symptoms:

- Pain in the abdomen. *Check*

- Chills, dehydration, dizziness, fatigue, fever, lightheadedness, loss of appetite, malaise, or sweating. *Check*

- Bloating, diarrhea, gagging, indigestion, nausea, vomiting, flatulence, or stomach cramps. *Check*

- Headache or weakness. *Check* and *Check*

My pilgrim partner was miserable, and I was miserable for him.

A bowl of this and you'll positively trot down the Camino.
(Takeaway, CC BY-SA 3.0, via Wikimedia Commons)

It was a bright, crisp day for walking. The first seventeen kilometers was without a town of any kind, though an enterprising young couple set up a food truck in a farmer's field at which we stopped for coffee. Well, we

both stopped but Craig passed on the coffee, not wishing to risk assaulting his tender tummy.

Long views, few towns. (José Antonio Gil Martínez from Vigo, Spain, CC BY 2.0, via Wikimedia Commons)

We chatted from time to time that morning with Lu, Rainbow, and Gayle—a British woman living in France. Gayle was walking the Camino with some girlfriends. Their husbands were driving a swanky van and lugging the ladies' gear. They also met them at various crossroads for picnics of French red wine and wee nibbles designed to keep body and soul together.

As we walked along it was clear that Craig was still suffering significant GI distress. From time to time I observed him sneaking into the bushes to unload more of the previous night's supper. I explained to Gayle that Craig was ill and that I was worried about him. It is hard enough to walk twenty miles. Walking twenty miles while vomiting is, well, a herculean task. Might she be willing to convince her group's menfolk to give Craig a ride up the road to the *albergue* where we planned to spend the night? Certainly. She would be delighted. As would the menfolk. But Craig is as mentally tough as he is physically hardy. He declined the ride, determined to cover every inch of the Camino on his own two feet. We can now add to the Mayo Clinic's list "poor judgment" and "excessive stubbornness." *Check* and *Check*.

Though we were scheduled to walk twenty miles to Moratinos, we decided to quit about three kilometers early in Terradillos de Los Templarios before Craig's energy—very low at the start of the day—flagged completely. We checked into Albergue los Templarios there and hoped that we would be able to push on to Calzadilla de los Hermanillos in the morning.

We paid an extra two euros for a smaller bunkroom that had a private bathroom. After we settled in—well, I settled in—Craig collapsed on his bunk and did not move for the next fifteen hours, Anna and Trevor from Brisbane, Australia came in to claim the other two bunks. I explained that Craig was ill, but they took it in stride and were charming bunkroom companions whose company we would enjoy all the way to Santiago de Compostela.

We met a couple of new pilgrims in the Terradillos *albergue*. Emily was a student from Minnesota who had just completed her first day on the Camino. Susan was a sixtysomething art professor from the Rhode Island School of Design. She was painting her way across Spain. I had plenty of time to talk with these new pilgrims and some of the more established members of our pilgrim bubble as I let Craig slumber in silence in the bunkroom.

I was able to renew my attention with respect to the deeper purposes of this pilgrimage as I whiled away the spare hours in the fading springtime sunlight. The gratitude I felt at being released from the cloying anger that tormented me three years before was profound indeed. Each person I met on the pilgrimage seemed to me to be heaven-sent, and reminded me of God's goodness. Cædmon said it better than I can:

> Now we must honor heaven-kingdom's Guardian,
> the might of the Architect and his mind-plans,
> the work of the Glory-Father. First he, the eternal Lord,
> established the foundation of wonders.
> Then he, the first Poet, created heaven as a roof
> for the sons of men, holy Creator,
> Guardian of mankind. Then he, the eternal Lord,
> afterwards made the middle earth for men, Master almighty.[3]

3. The earliest Old English poem still extant today is probably "Cædmon's Hymn," a lyric of praise, gratitude, and thanksgiving which was composed sometime between AD 658 and 680. According to the scholar Bede (673–735), Cædmon was an illiterate herdsman who worked at the monastery of Whitby, a small English fishing village. Cædmon, according to the Venerable Bede, was given the gift of poetic composition by an angel. ("Cædmon's Hymn").

Chapter 19

Terradillos de los Templarios to Calzadilla de los Hermanillos

O Lord my God, make me quick-witted without flippancy.
— *Aquinas, Aquinas Prayer Book*

C RAIG's stomach illness seemed to have abated by the morning. He slept most of the afternoon and all night. The vomiting had stopped and he claimed a renewed interest in food. We were on the path by 6:15 with my new headlamp purchased in Carriòn de los Condes, though it should be noted that there was very little to bump into that morning. The walk between Terradillos and Calzadilla was about half road walking and half through the countryside, with the promise of a midpoint stop in Sahagún, population 2,800. The thought of a place so heavily populated—by Camino standards—allowed our imaginations to soar to previously unexplored heights. Perhaps we would see Sahagún rise from the prairie like a veritable Emerald City.

We enjoyed a nice chat with a sports physical therapist from Latvia. Ilona was an engaging conversation partner, though there was a certain aura of melancholy about her. She confessed to feeling a deep ache caused by the separation from her two young children and her husband—understandably.

I could sympathize with the pain of homesickness for hearth and home, kith and kin.

We ran into Harold from Mauritius and Ira from Finland at our first coffee stop. Both were just the most delightful people with seemingly permanent wide smiles. Craig's tummy seemed to handle the coffee break well.

We discussed our León itinerary while walking that day. We agreed that we would stay the next night in Mansilla de las Mulas, then walk eleven miles into León on Wednesday. We would get a hotel there, see whatever sights we could on Wednesday afternoon and evening, then leave León on Thursday morning. While this would not give us the full rest day we had originally planned, we both agreed that we did not need a break yet. This would also give us a jump on getting to Santiago in time to greet Carol and Dar when they arrived. And by that point in our pilgrimage, we had begun to think of an eleven-mile day as a rest day.

Craig "the Smiling" and Alfonso VI "the Brave" pose near Sahagún,
the Camino's halfway point.

Eventually we finished our seventeen-mile walk to Calzadilla de los Hermanillos. It was a sleepy little place out in the boondocks. Actually, I am not sure if the boondocks have ever heard of it. If it is to be found among the places worthy of boondock status, it is a footnote at best. We were the first pilgrims to arrive. Since the *albergue* did not open for another hour we bought groceries for our lunch and the next day's breakfast at the small market next door and chilled out on a bench on the sunny sidewalk.

Our Terradillos roommates—Trevor and Anna—were also in our *albergue* that night. Trevor offered to cook for the four of us. He prepared pasta laced with tomato, zucchini, and spicy chorizo sausage. Anna provided flan for dessert. We enjoyed the meal and the conversation very much. We traded contact information and have stayed in touch since returning from the Camino.

The *albergue* was thinly populated by a French couple and two German women. We were grateful for our lower bunks.

We met Flow and Mo coming out of the small grocery next to our *albergue*. Flow delighted us with breathless accounts of the news of all that she and Mo had experienced since our last chat in Zariquiegui.

The next day's walk to Mansilla de las Mulas would begin with a seventeen-kilometer walk through the countryside along the old Roman road—the *Via Trajana*. We anticipated being ready for a cup of coffee by the time we arrived at our first town—Reliegos.

We passed the halfway point that day. We reckoned that we had about fifteen days to go. I was very grateful.

Chapter 20

Calzadilla de los Hermanillos to Mansilla de las Mulas

O Lord my God, let me fear You without losing hope.
— Aquinas, Aquinas Prayer Book

W E enjoyed a good night of rest, though my neck was acting up a bit, as it does from time to time. A couple of days sleeping with a flat pillow would take care of the problem. We left Calzadilla around 6:15. Within thirty minutes or so the eastern sky began to brighten and provided a terrific sunrise set against the few trees of the *meseta*. Daylight also revealed the distant mountains to our north and west. We would be climbing up and over those western ranges beginning in a week or less.

The *meseta* was alive with birdsong that morning. The first few hours of the walk were utterly devoid of human habitation of any kind, so the natural sounds of the prairie were magnified. It was lovely. There were no paved roads carrying vehicles at speed to urgent destinations. There were no trains ferrying day-laborers to their assigned tasks. There was no built environment imposing on creation. There was only light, grass, wind, and birdsong. Bessie Rayner Parkes might have captured it thus:

Sweet melody amidst the moving spheres
Breaks forth, a solemn and entrancing sound,
A harmony whereof the earth's green hills
Give but the faintest echo; yet is there
A music everywhere, and concert sweet!
All birds which sing amidst the forest deep
Till the flowers listen with unfolded bells;
All winds that murmur over summer grass,
Or curl the waves upon the pebbly shore;
Chiefly all earnest human voices rais'd
In charity and for the cause of truth,
Mingle together in one sacred chord,
And float, a grateful incense, up to God.[1]

Among the birds we heard that day and most days were cuckoos. I had not seen one as far as I knew, but we heard them all the time. Their "cuckoo" song was as regular and clear as the clocks named for them. It turns out that the cuckoo is an interesting bird. Perhaps you will fascinate your conversation partners at the next cocktail party with these nuggets of cuckoo knowledge:[2]

- Migrating north from Africa, the first male common cuckoos ('cuckoos') reach Europe in mid-April. In the minds of most country people, spring only truly arrives when the first cuckoo call is heard

- The cuckoo is a brood parasite. It is well-known for its habit of laying an egg in the nest of another bird, then leaving the offspring to be hatched and fed by 'foster parents'. This cunning tactic allows for more young cuckoos to be reared than would otherwise be possible.[3]

- The cuckoo has long been associated with fate for humans. Numerous beliefs exist, including: it is good luck to have money in your pocket when you hear a cuckoo; whatever you are doing when you hear a cuckoo, you should repeat throughout the year as the call was a sign that the particular activity will be beneficial; for single people, the number of calls or notes would signify how many years they would

1. Parkes, *Poems*, 105.

2. "Amazing Facts about the Cuckoo."

3. Recent evidence suggests that brood parasites like the cuckoo choose their host nests based on the eye size of the host parents. The smaller the eyes—and the weaker the eyesight—the more likely that the hosts won't recognize the cuckoo's eggs as foreign. (Ausprey and Hauber, "Host and Brood Parasite," 1

remain unmarried; and in Sweden, the direction of the call signifies either good luck (west), death (south), consolation (east), or sorrow (north).

Hard to see. Easy to hear. (Afsarnayakkan, CC BY-SA 3.0, via Wikimedia Commons)

I received an email from Josh and Bianka letting us know that they were a few days ahead of us. They planned to fly out of Santiago on June 5 and were hoping for a meet-up there if we arrived soon enough. It would be fun to see them again, and we hoped we would get the chance.

The day's walk was hard for me. It was very flat, but the first section was soooo long, and the path was quite stony. I felt better after we finally reached Reliegos and had coffee and toast. From there it was only six kilometers into Mansilla de las Mulas.

The walk that morning was so very flat that I feel compelled to comment briefly here on the nature of flatness. It turns out that there is more than meets the eye when it comes to flatness. There is, for example, the common expression "flat as a pancake," about which Ammer has this to say:

> "Flat as a Pancake": Exceedingly flat, sometimes excessively so. This simile has been around since the sixteenth century, appearing in Nicholas Udall's translation of Erasmus (1542) and Henry Porter's play The Two Angrie Women of Abington. Moreover, it

survived and replaced the equally old "flat as a flounder" and is still frequently used today . . .[4]

Scientists have actually studied (for reasons surpassing understanding) whether certain prairie land masses are indeed "flat as a pancake." In what must certainly rank as one of modernity's more egregious scientific wastes of time, Mark Fonstad et al.[5] sought to determine whether the US state of Kansas was flatter than a pancake. It turns out that it is flatter—and quite a bit so. Indeed, the lofty peaks of the average pancake are positively *alpine* compared to Kansas. Fascinating.

Flat? Hardly. (Shisma, CC BY 4.0, via Wikimedia Commons)

But there are other ways to define flatness:

- *Commercially inactive.* This works. There wasn't much commerce on the *meseta*.

- *Not reflecting light.* Well, I am not sure that the *meseta* reflects much light, but it was bright and sunny that day.

- *Having a relatively broad surface in relation to depth or thickness.* I have no idea how thick the *meseta* is, so I do not really know if this definition applies.

- *Lacking contrast or shading between tones.* Nope. The variation in color and sound was, if anything, enhanced in this prairie setting.

---

4. "Flat as a Pancake," s.v. https://idioms.thefreedictionary.com/flat+as+a+pancake.
5. APS News, "Zero Gravity."

- *Lacking stimulating characteristics.* Hmmm . . . no. There was nature aplenty to stimulate the senses.

- *Lacking taste or flavor or tang.* I suppose the dirt of the *meseta* tastes about the same as the dirt of the Pyrenees, so this definition won't do.[6]

Was the *meseta* flat? You decide.

The fenced, preserved *Via Trajana*. We walked to the left.
The Romans walked to the right. It was very flat.

We had made a reservation at Albergue Gaia, where *hospitaleros* Maria and Carlos had taken such good care of Joe and me in 2016. They welcomed us warmly, and were even able to find my name in their register for October 1, 2016. I felt like a time-traveler.

We had a drink outside the bar next to the *albergue* while we waited for the house to open. Craig kept an eye on our packs while I strolled down to the farmers' market that was in full swing in the central plaza. I bought lettuce, red pepper, tomatoes, cucumber, cheese, and cherries for our do-it-yourself dinner that evening. I stopped in the small grocery store on the

6. "Flat." s.v. https://www.thefreedictionary.com/flat.

way back to see if they would sell me a couple of eggs to hard-boil for the salad, but the proprietor would only sell me six. I passed, but was delighted to find some eggs in the *albergue's* kitchen. Maria encouraged us to use them for our meal.

Mansilla had a wonderful pilgrim-themed sculpture across the street from the *albergue*. Three weary pilgrims in various postures of physical and mental fatigue rest at the foot of the cross. It was a good reminder for me of what the pilgrimage was for.

Craig and I could relate. (DoctorMaligno, Public domain, via Wikimedia Commons)

Craig and I had a nice chat with Chelsea from Colorado on the *albergue's* patio. She had a kind of New Age hippie worldview, but seemed very open to others, and was a lively and engaging conversation partner. She was excited to share her plans for opening a retreat center that would feature yurts, vegetarian cuisine, and guided meditations enhanced by psychedelic mushrooms. While I have always wondered what living in a yurt was like, I do enjoy the occasional cheeseburger. Hold the mushrooms. I do not think Chelsea's retreat center is for me.

I had a funny encounter with some French pilgrims in the *albergue's* bunkroom. There was a group of perhaps six *pèlerins* in their late sixties or early seventies walking the Camino together. One of the ladies had the lower bunk next to my lower bunk. The beds were fairly close together, and as we both bent over to arrange our sleeping sacks we bumped bottoms and tumbled headfirst into our respective bunks. We had a good-natured laugh about it, and for the rest of the day she referred to me as *Monsieur Derrière*. The ironic thing about it is that Carol often refers to me in the Anglicized form of this *surnom affectueux*: Mr. Ass.

We went to Mass in the church to end our day. As is so common in many Spanish churches, imagery related to Mary was very present, while Jesus was a bit harder to locate. This was disappointing to me, but consistent with what I had seen in Spain on both of my pilgrimages. Devotion to Mary is very strong in Spain, and is a central, defining element of Spanish culture, indeed of all Spanish-speaking cultures the world over.[7]

Blessed Solanus Casey encourages us to "thank God ahead of time." This was good advice as I drifted off to sleep after another good day, with gratitude for the day to come.

7. Hall, *Mary, Mother and Warrior,* 3.

Chapter 21

Mansilla de las Mulas to León

O Lord my God, let me be truthful without guile.
— *Aquinas, Aquinas Prayer Book*

W<small>E</small> got our usual early morning start. The bunkroom at the *albergue* was very warm and stuffy in the night. It was good to breathe fresh air as we walked in the crisp morning air.

Our walk took us through a few small towns that form the outermost ring of the larger León metro area. Eventually we entered a zone of industrial and commercial activity before finding our way into the city proper. León is like most other major cities with ancient roots. The old town is charming, interesting, and exciting. The Way leading into and out of the old town is gritty, commercial, and is simply to be endured.

We shared a table at our first coffee break with Johan from the Netherlands. We had seen him from time to time along the Camino. At the Santa Maria del Camino *albergue* in Carrión we learned that he was walking The Way in memory of his recently deceased wife. He shared more of his story during our coffee break, including experience of being fired from his university administrator position after many decades of service. I could relate to his disappointment in this.

It was Craig's turn to buy coffee and breakfast that morning. He asked if I wanted toast (as usual). The bar had a piece of "meat pie" in the case and I expressed a preference for that. It was delicious, and if it was not for the fact that I would likely die early from heart disease, I'd eat it every day.

This looked better to me than toast. (Tamorlan, CC BY 3.0, via Wikimedia Commons)

I stopped at a sports store on our way into the city center to buy some new socks. Two of the socks that began the pilgrimage on their last legs finally sprouted holes. I hoped that switching styles of socks might help with chronic problems I was experiencing with toe blisters. I ended up buying a couple of pairs of thin socks that I thought might give my toes a bit more space. This turned out to be a poor choice. Blisters continued. I threw the socks away when I reached Santiago de Compostela.

Once we entered León proper we were greeted by a group of pilgrim-welcomers who provided us with sweet treats, maps of the city, *albergue* suggestions, and other helpful advice. They were retired folks who had walked the Camino and derived satisfaction from being of assistance to present-day pilgrims. This is just one more example of the thick hospitality we experienced every day on the Camino de Santiago.

Once we located our accommodation—the Hotel Real Colegiata San Isidoro—we checked our packs behind the counter and headed to the cathedral for a look-around. It was a soaring monument to stained glass. It was very different from the Burgos Cathedral, but was simply beautiful in its own way.

Our León digs.

We had some time to kill before our room would be ready so we strolled through the farmers market in the main plaza. A vendor gave me a nectarine which was (1) juicy and (2) delicious. Craig bought us peaches that were (1) hard as rocks and (2) tasteless. If used as baseballs, the players would go through a lot of bats. As my sainted mother said many times, "It's the thought that counts."

León Cathedral. My goodness.

Our hotel was connected to the basilica of the same name. It was very nice for the price and used to be a monastery. We looked forward to sleeping without the usual inconveniences associated with *albergues*. I practiced sleeping that afternoon and it was a delight.

Hard peaches sold here. (Txo, CC BY-SA 3.0, via Wikimedia Commons)

The best part of the day was a phone call with Carol. We were both counting the days until we would be reunited in Santiago de Compostela.

I went to Mass in the cathedral, and then met Craig for dinner at a nice restaurant in the cathedral square. We ran into Kerstin from Sweden, Rainbow from Pennsylvania, and Ann and Carl from Sweden. We had seen Kerstin from time to time in various towns and villages, including Terradillos where we shared the same *albergue*. That evening in León she was experiencing some troubles occasioned by the loss of her credit card. Craig and I bought her dinner so her cash would extend a bit longer until she could get things sorted out with her bank back in Sweden. She was a delightful person, and I have enjoyed staying in touch with her from time to time since returning home from the Camino.

We would have a twenty-mile walk after leaving León, so it was off to bed after our delightful dinner. The 5:00 alarm was coming for us.

Chapter 22

León to Villavante

O Lord my God, let me do good works without presumption
— Aquinas, Aquinas Prayer Book.

B ECAUSE we had such a long walk, we awoke at 5:00 and were navigating the way out of León by 5:30. We were able to find all the yellow arrows, which was not so easy in a darkened city.

We walked from Fresno del Camino to Chozas de Abajo with Neri. We first encountered Neri in Carrión de los Condes a few days before. She became separated from her six friends who somehow took the alternate path at Virgen del Camino where the concrete of Greater León stops abruptly and the dirt paths of the countryside resume. She would catch up with them in Hospital de Orbigo where the routes merged again. She was a delightful person who confided that she felt complete in her life except for the spiritual fulfillment she had gradually lost over the years. We had a good chat about that part of her life, and I gave her a rosary to help her recapture a spirit of prayer during what remained of the Camino.

La Basilica de la Virgen del Camino in morning shadow.
(David Perez, CC BY 3.0, via Wikimedia Commons)

We walked behind a couple from Spokane. I was told he did twenty-five push-ups every mile. For you math aficionados that's 12,500 push-ups over the course of the Camino. My push-up total was somewhat lower. They were pleasant folks, but man, that's a lot of push-ups.

For a time as we approached Villavante we walked behind, then with, and eventually ahead of 200 sheep, two shepherds, and four sheepdogs. I sent a video home that I hoped the grandkids would enjoy.

We shared The Way with these hoofed pilgrims. (Peter O'Connor, aka anemoneprojectors, CC BY-SA 2.0, via Wikimedia Commons)

Sheep husbandry and the worldwide wool economy it supported were hugely important and influential in Spain for centuries.[1] But like any monoculture, such lack of agricultural diversity has negative consequences. Sheep are voracious eaters and will devour any plant material made available to them. They are thought to be a principal cause of deforestation of the *meseta*:

> The sheep raising nobility had in late medieval and early modern Spain a dominance of politics and the economy of the type Texas oil plutocrats enjoy in the United States. All of the interests of the state were focused on their needs and demands, and they had the ability to dictate government policies. The landed nobility controlled vast expanses of land, and some of the best endowed among them had estates in several parts of Spain. Their wealth was overwhelmingly from the sale of fleece, and thus their demands were for freedom from government regulation of the wool trade, except where such regulation was beneficial to the profits they expected from that trade. They wanted, and got, rights to exploit vast areas of land beyond their estates, lands nominally held by the state or held in common by the populace, and they wanted that usage to be free from competition from other users. When there was a conflict, the sheep raisers were the de facto winners in almost all situations. A farmer attempting to grow a crop next to one of the sheep runs might complain that sheep wandering off the runs ate his growing crop, but that was as far as it could go, a complaint, for the sheep owners were held harmless. They were well organized, initially in locally based mestas to control sheep runs and eventually in the Council of the Mesta, a large state-within-a-state entity. The Mesta ran its own courts to adjudicate disputes between various owners of herds and between those owners and landowners with plots adjacent to the sheep runs. It was rare indeed for the latter to win disputes, especially as the Mesta had tremendous influence with the royal household. The export of fleece was the source of the income of the nobility and they, in turn, supported the government through loans and levies. For that support they had the ear and the backing of royalty and government. It was willing to formulate its policies to encourage the trade in wool, and

---

1. Even now herders have rights to drive their flocks from northern pastures to winter grazing lands along 78,000 miles of protected *sendas*. In 1994, shepherds began herding their flocks through metropolitan Madrid, turning the annual migration into a fiesta, with thousands lining the streets to observe the ritual. ("Sheep Replace Cars").

on occasion it was willing to wage war to meet the demands of its wool-producing members.[2]

Indeed, so highly prized was the merino wool that comprised the Spanish monopoly that laws were promulgated forbidding the export of such sheep outside of Spain. Penalties were severe, including capital punishment. Beheadings notwithstanding, the English and French eventually managed to steal enough breeding stock to end the Spanish monopoly in the eighteenth century.

Our encounter with the sheep delighted me. But I was also reminded that day—as I am every day that I'm separated from Carol—that my heart lies with her everywhere and always:

> Come live with me and be my love,
> And we will all the pleasures prove,
> That Valleys, groves, hills, and fields,
> Woods, or steepy mountain yields.
> And we will sit upon the Rocks,
> Seeing the Shepherds feed their flocks,
> By shallow Rivers to whose falls
> Melodious birds sing Madrigals.
> And I will make thee beds of Roses
> And a thousand fragrant posies,
> A cap of flowers, and a kirtle
> Embroidered all with leaves of Myrtle;
> A gown made of the finest wool
> Which from our pretty Lambs we pull;
> Fair lined slippers for the cold,
> With buckles of the purest gold;
> A belt of straw and Ivy buds,
> With Coral clasps and Amber studs:
> And if these pleasures may thee move,
> Come live with me, and be my love.
> The Shepherds' Swains shall dance and sing
> For thy delight each May-morning:
> If these delights thy mind may move,
> Then live with me, and be my love.[3]

We encountered a pilgrim who passed us going the wrong way. When I pointed out that Santiago was in the opposite direction, he pointed east

---

2. Pederson, "Sheep and the Camino," 3-4.
3. Marlowe, *Passionate Shepherd*, 11–16, 207.

and shouted "Roma!" He had already walked from Rome to Santiago and now was walking back. My pilgrimage felt puny by comparison.

There was a class of thirteen students from Boston College in our *albergue* in Villavante. They had just begun their *camino* in León that day, and were taking a philosophy course with their professor while they walked.[4] They were still full of energy, and brought an atmosphere of youthful exuberance to the *albergue*. We also met Ralph from Munich who also began his *camino* in León. We ate dinner with him in the *albergue* and enjoyed his company very much.

The blisters I had been experiencing were typically of the nagging, minor variety. They were limited to my toes, and while irritating, were easily managed. Unfortunately, Craig was beginning to suffer from more serious blisters, especially on his heel. His shoes—which had served him so well during the 700 miles or so we walked during our training—were beginning to deteriorate.[5] Our route from Villvante to Astorga would only be about twelve miles. We hoped a shorter day would help Craig's grumpy feet.

I was counting down the days until I could see Carol. They could not come soon enough. My ache to be reunited with her put me in mind of something the author Katherine Mansfield[6] once wrote to John Middleton Murry:

> My love for you tonight is so deep and tender that it seems to be outside myself as well. I am fast shut up like a little lake in the embrace of some big mountains. If you were to climb up the mountains, you would see me down below, deep and shining—and quite fathomless, my dear. You might drop your heart into me and you'd never hear it touch bottom.

4. Jason, "Deliberate Walk."

5. According to legend, Sts Crispin and Crispinian traveled from Rome to the French town of Soissons, where they preached and earned a living as shoemakers, offering shoes to the poor at a very low price and using leather provided by angels. The people of Soissons built a church in their honor in the sixth century, and since that time they have been known as the patron saints of shoemakers and other workers in leather. People who wore shoes that were too tight were said to be "in St. Crispin's prison" (Ordish, *St. Crispin's Day*, 137–144.).

6. Tabori and Tabori Fried, *Little Book of Love Poems*, 56.

Chapter 23

Villavante to Astorga

O Lord my God, let me rebuke my neighbor without haughtiness, and—without
hypocrisy—strengthen him by word and example.
— Aquinas, Aquinas Prayer Book

W E walked into Astorga with Oliver from Passau, who biked from
home to St. Jean and walked from there. He'd had quite a journey
up to that point.

We missed TWO alternate routes that morning and ended up walking
to Astorga along the busy, noisy highway. We had done this a couple of
times—including our walk into Burgos. I hoped that I would have learned
a lesson: pay better attention to the yellow arrows and do not follow blindly
behind other pilgrims. Well, I am a slow learner, evidently.

In addition to the Boston College students we met at the *albergue*
in Villvante, there was a second group from Valparaiso University in the
Astorga *albergue*. Both groups were taking travel courses on pilgrimage and
related topics. I spoke with the Valparaiso professor—David Weber—who,
as it turned out, is a former colleague of my college's dean. We spoke a bit
about his course and my Senior Seminar. It is a pretty small world. He wrote

an article on the pilgrimage experience with his students after returning from the Camino.[1]

The walk into Astorga was thirsty work.

We ate dinner in Astorga's central plaza on what turned out to be a lovely evening, though it was a bit breezy. Two ladies enjoying an early evening coffee were knocked in the head by a windblown restaurant patio umbrella of considerable size. Fortunately, there was no lasting damage. It was a weekend, and as the sun slipped below the rooflines Astorga's families began to trickle into the square. Face painting, music, dancing, and family games ensued, and a very good time was had by all—locals and visitors alike.

We shared a bunk room with Neri from Los Angeles and Kathleen Graham—a delightful Kiwi artist we'd seen from time to time. Kath was horrified by my toes and their sorry state of health. I assured her that the painful days were—I hoped—behind me. Still, she plied me with lamb's wool and other home remedies popular among New Zealanders. I responded gratefully enough for her to give me a couple of her watercolor bookmarks, which are very nice.

1. Weber, *Buen Camino.*

We toured Astorga's cathedral and Gaudí's episcopal palace—originally built as the bishop's residence but now a museum dedicated to the Camino pilgrimage. Both were magnificent, though these experiences did force me to ask myself, "When is a pilgrim a tourist?" This is a question asked by those interested in pilgrimage the world over. Are those who walk (or ride?) to shrines or other religious sites *merely* pilgrims? Do they have touristic tendencies, even if they do not think of themselves as tourists? Does it matter, and if so, in what ways? Scholars take this question seriously, with some asserting that the two categories are always and everywhere separable.[2] Rhodes College professor Thomas Bremer (citing the historian Peter Brown) has this to say on the subject:

> The eminent historian of the early Christian world Peter Brown once remarked that the difference between pilgrimage and tourism has to do with the worthiness of the traveler. Pilgrims, he explained, go on their journeys to make themselves worthy to experience *praesentia*, the physical presence of the saint. They spend days, weeks, months, sometimes years, enduring the hardships of travel in an effort to transform themselves into individuals worthy of the sacramental presence that they experience at their destination. Pilgrims' travels, at least ideally in Christian practice, amount to an exercise in humility, dedication, and faith. The hardships they undergo purge pilgrims of their worldly pleasures and offer them an ascetic focus on the sacred power entombed in the holy precincts of the pilgrimage destination.
>
> In contrast, tourists travel with an attitude of entitlement. They enter holy grounds as consumers of the sacred, rather than as humble souls worthy of the sacred presence, although, as we will see, many tourists at religious sites delight in consuming the aesthetic experience of sacred power. Caught up more in the logic of modern capitalism than in the ascetic demands of religious exchange, tourists expect an experience worthy of their expenditure of time, money, and energy. Thus, whereas the pilgrim seeks a self worthy of the experience, the tourist seeks experiences worthy of the self.[3]

It is reasonable to assert that most twenty-first-century pilgrims—even if religiously devout and committed to a spirit of spiritual renewal—have a difficult time avoiding the consumer attractions that form the economic

2. Palmer et al., "In Defense of Differentiating Pilgrimage from Tourism," 71–85.

3. Bremer, "Touristic Spirit," 2:37.

basis of modern pilgrimage. And while this distinction is perhaps more obvious in modernity, medieval pilgrims likely experienced the same tendencies as demonstrated by the badges and other souvenirs they commonly brought home following arrival at a shrine. Perhaps this is why some late medieval and early modern religious thinkers discouraged pilgrimage—indeed, nonessential travel of any kind. Perhaps Craig and I were pilgrims with touristic tendencies. We were real pilgrims, doing our

best to be worthy of the spiritual blessings of the pilgrimage, who enjoyed what we saw and took advantage of various creature comforts available to us along The Way. I can't speak for Craig, but I can live with myself, for it is the trying that matters.

Medieval pilgrims to St. James with souvenir scallop shells on their hats. (Lucas van Leyden, *Resting Pilgrims*, Public domain, via Wikimedia Commons)

I did not think anything could get any better for Craig after the funeral that he stumbled upon in Villamayor de Monjardín. Until, that is, we walked out of the Astorga cathedral and spotted a funeral in process right across the street. Craig—shod in flip-flops with lavishly bandaged, leprous feet—positively sprinted across the street to get a better view. Christmas Day came early for Craig.

A Spanish funeral. Every pilgrim's dream.

The next day would take us back up into the high country and away from the plains that had shaped our environment for the previous ten days. While I looked forward to the change of scenery, I knew from experience that tired legs, sore knees, and burning lungs were going to be the new normal. I fell asleep that night cognizant of Pope St. John Paul II's advice:[4]

> *Duc in altum!* These words ring out for us today, and they invite us to remember the past with gratitude, to live the present with enthusiasm, and to look forward to the future with confidence.

4. John Paul II, "*Novo Millennio Ineunte*," 2.

Chapter 24

Astorga to Foncebadón

Give to me, O Lord God, a watchful heart,
which no capricious thought can lure away from You.
— Aquinas, Aquinas Prayer Book

WHILE we enjoyed a fine day in Astorga, it was good to get moving around 6:00 as we snuck out of town past the cathedral, the Episcopal Palace, and Craig's favorite place on the entire Camino—the Emilio "*El Pertiguero*" funeral home.

The walk that morning was flat-to-gently-uphill until we reached Santa Catalina where the earth tipped and it was all uphill until we reached Foncebadón around 1:00. We stopped for coffee a couple of times. At our first stop a pilgrim came up to me and asked if I had a knife she could use. Her name was Nona and she was a Russian physics professor now living and working as a real estate agent in Seattle. She skedaddled from Moscow with her kids because she feared their conscription in the Russian army in which, according to her understanding, "99.9 percent of soldiers die." While I doubt the statistics are quite so grim, I give her credit for having the fortitude to make such a drastic change to safeguard her children. What did she need my knife for? She had been carrying a sausage of substantial heft around for a couple of days with no way to cut it up. She carved it up then and there and it was a delicious adjunct to our *cafe con leche* and croissant.

Along the way we ran into Harold from Mauritius again. This guy was fascinating. Of French heritage, he went to college in South Africa and led the biggest business in his Indian Ocean island nation—a garment-manufacturing concern that employs 18,000 people in four countries. A very devout fellow, we saw him often at Mass in the various towns through which we passed. He told us of his plans to retire in a few months after thirty years with the company to devote himself to a nonprofit he started called Lovebridge.[1] It partners the poor with social workers to accompany and befriend them to combat poverty in Mauritius. As he described this work, I could see how intensely it animated him and his devotion to the people of his country who will benefit from it. Had St. Augustine been walking The Way with Harold, he might have had this to say about him and Lovebridge:

> What sort of face has love? What form has it? What stature? What feet? What hands has it? No man can say. And yet it has feet, for these carry men to church: it has hands; for these reach forth to the poor: it has eyes; for thereby we consider the needy: Blessed is the man, it is said, who considers the needy and the poor. It has ears, of which the Lord says, He that has ears to hear let him hear.[2]

Some people have the gift of conveying a genuine interest in whatever their conversation partner has to say. They make contact with their eyes. Their faces are expressive, and respond to new facts, insights, and observations as if these were precious jewels worthy of rapt attention. Their body language suggests a real interest in what they are hearing. So it was with Harold. I recall an example from when we stayed together in the Santa Brigida *albergue* in Hontanas. It was a chilly evening, and I was concerned that my sleeping bag liner would not suffice. As the *hospitalero* asked me to follow him to another part of the house to find blankets I asked Harold if he would like me to bring one back for him. He boomed in response "With pleasure!" He could have simply said "yes" or "thank you" or offered an endless range of diminutive affirmations. But that was not his style. "With pleasure!" suited him much better. Every conversation we had after that displayed this zest for the present. We traded contact information, and I looked forward to staying in touch with him.

1. https://www.lovebridge.mu/en.
2. Augustine, "Homily 7 on the First Epistle of John," para. 11.

Craig and Harold take a break on the climb to Foncebadón.

The wildflowers on the hillsides approaching Foncebadón were stunningly beautiful. Reds, purples, bright yellows, and brilliant whites covered the green shrubbery. This showy brilliance was such a difference from my 2016 experience when everything was dry and brown.

The wildflowers in the mountains were beautiful. (Bureau of Reclamation, CC BY-SA 2.0, via Wikimedia Commons)

We continued to book *albergues* a few days ahead because there were a lot of pilgrims out there. I was not sure if it was absolutely necessary to book ahead, for Craig and I were early risers and often among the first pilgrims to arrive at our destination. Still, knowing that we had a place to lay our heads at night made walking during the day a more enjoyable and stress-free experience.

We reckoned that we had nine days of walking left, and hoped to arrive in Santiago—God willing—on June 3. My legs were tired but we were anxious to arrive in Santiago before Carol and Dar so we could greet them at the airport. We had started to give some thought to where Craig and I would stay in Santiago until the ladies arrived and we moved into the hotel we had booked many months before.

The rough-but-beautiful climb to Foncebadón.

Craig's feet were bothering him more with each passing day, but my toenail blisters were drying up nicely and did not bother me at all on our walk from Astorga. I was very grateful. Blisters—or indeed any foot problems—have a way of enslaving one's every thought. Some bodily complaints tend to fade from consciousness as tissues warm with exercise. Not so, blisters. Not so. Blisters are like tongues of flame that increase in temperature and scope with each successive step. Soon the victim's vision narrows. The normally pleasant sounds of the natural world dull and are replaced by a discordant roaring. The easy gait of a pilgrim unencumbered by enforced worldly responsibility gradually stiffens as the walker is transformed into a limping, crabbed, Gollum-like figure. Even the most cheerfully optimistic pilgrim takes on the countenance of a migraine-sufferer when blisters join him or her on the Camino. God save us all from this plague.

Can't have a pilgrim memoir without a blister photo. Sorry.

The next day, at Cruz de Ferro, I would lay down the stones and the burdens they represent for the nearly thirty people who were on my prayer list during this pilgrimage. I was looking forward to lightening my spirit—and my backpack—by doing so.

Chapter 25

Foncebadón to Ponferrada

Give to me, O Lord God, a noble heart,
which no unworthy desire can debase.
— *Aquinas, Aquinas Prayer Book*

T HE Foncebadón bunkroom was a snoratorium populated by members of the International Brotherhood of Coughers and Noseblowers. Needless to say, I did not enjoy my best sleep. It was not the worst, but it was far from the best. Plus, it was an aged group—early to bed and early to rise. The good people of Bunkroom Number One were up and at 'em by 5:00. By 5:15 I figured I may as well join them.

The walk to Cruz de Ferro required our headlamps. The thirty-minute climb through the inky darkness with a million stars twinkling high above the mountain path was warming as the cold breeze ruffled jacket sleeves and pant legs. The eastern horizon began to brighten as we rounded a rise in the path and got our first glimpse of the Cruz de Ferro perched atop its cairn of a million pilgrims' stones. I climbed to the top of the small hill, said a prayer, and laid down the stones I'd been carrying for others since the pilgrimage began. I also laid one down for those in my family whose struggles merited an extra prayer or two. It was a very significant moment for which I remain grateful. Stones deposited, burdens laid down, gratitude expressed, and prayers offered, we looked briefly at the brightening horizon and pointed our faces west toward Ponferrada, and beyond that, to Santiago de Compostela.

Pilgrims can find hospitality at Manjarín in the lonely Irago Mountains.
(Jonathan Jacobi, CC BY-SA 3.0, via Wikimedia Commons)

The rising sun's backlighting rendered the wildflowers gorgeous. Bright whites, yellows, purples, and vivid reds carpeted the mountain path. I wish I was a better photographer so I could have captured it. The natural beauty of the place put me in mind of Robert Louis Stevenson's ode to the natural wonder of the Scottish highlands:

> In the highlands, in the country places,
> Where the old plain men have rosy faces,
>   And the young fair maidens
>   Quiet eyes;
> Where essential silence cheers and blesses,
> And for ever in the hill-recesses
>   Her more lovely music
>   Broods and dies—
> O to mount again where erst I haunted;
> Where the old red hills are bird-enchanted,
>   And the low green meadows
>   Bright with sward;
> And when even dies, the million-tinted,

And the night has come, and planets glinted,
> Lo, the valley hollow
>> Lamp-bestarr'd!
O to dream, O to awake and wander
There, and with delight to take and render,
> Through the trance of silence,
>> Quiet breath!
Lo! for there, among the flowers and grasses,
Only the mightier movement sounds and passes;
> Only winds and rivers,
>> Life and death.[1]

We could see Ponferrada in the valley in the distance. It did not look so far away. "Be there in a jiffy" we thought to ourselves. Well, it was, as an old friend was known to quip, "an optical delusion." And it was all steeply, knee-crunchingly, toe-bashingly downhill. For hours and hours. And hours. The path was littered with loose rocks—so much so that we eventually hopped onto the adjacent road and walked down the mountain on an engineered surface. Much better.

We stopped for coffee in El Acebo at a cafe run by a guy from Houston. He married a Spanish gal about ten years before and they settled down to run an *albergue* in this village of thirty-seven souls. His house was well located, for it was the first place that pilgrims descending the mountain could find refreshment after a long, tough walk. Craig and I both enjoyed a slice of *empanada* with our coffee. It tasted good and was good for us.

Coffee stop number two was in Molinaseca, at the foot of the Very Giant Steep Mountain. We shared a table with David Weber—the Valparaiso professor—and one of his students. I walked for a while with Sabrina, an Italian who spoke very little English and was equally deficient in Spanish. Still, we got by and had a good chat. We also kept running into Kath, with whom we shared a room in Astorga. She was good-natured, and we enjoyed our chats.

I sent an email to Sue and Brock, the Perth couple I met on the Camino in 2016. I thought of them often during my pilgrimage with Craig, and have enjoyed our long-distance friendship since our shared pilgrimage three years before.

Ponferrada was a frustrating town to enter. There are a few reasons for this. First, it comes at the end of a very long walk. We were utterly fatigued

---

1. Stevenson, *In the Highlands*, 212.

by the time we arrived. Second, the town sits in a river valley, and since we approached it from the top of a sizable mountain, we could see it but it seemed that we would never arrive. Finally, the *albergues*, main church, *plaza mayor*, and Templar castle were at the western end of the town, which was laid out along the river. The consequence of this is that once we actually—finally—made it to town, we had to walk a long way to get to the *albergue*. There were few days on the Camino when I was happier to finish the day's walk.

Ponferrada didn't look so far away from the top of those mountains.
(Zarateman, CC0, via Wikimedia Commons)

We went to the Mass in the Basilica Nuestra Senora de la Encina, which by Spanish standards is a relatively new church, being only 600 years old. We timed our arrival poorly and crept into the church just after the homily. The church was unusually full, though it was a Sunday and there was a concert after the Mass that was likely a draw for Ponferradans. There was a large group of people from Santiago, Chile visiting Ponferrada who attended the Mass in addition to the usual locals and pilgrims. After the Mass the priest invited all the pilgrims and the visitors from Chile to the front for a blessing.

Being Sunday, all the grocery stores were closed, which meant we needed to find a restaurant for dinner and abide until then on the cookies and oranges in our packs. We ended up enjoying a lovely, lively dinner in the plaza outside the basilica with Harold, Ira, Kieran, and Steph. After awhile Anna and Trevor joined us. It was lots of fun.

Chapter 26

Ponferrada to Villafranca del Bierzo

Give to me, O Lord God, a resolute heart,
which no evil intention can divert.
— *Aquinas, Aquinas Prayer Book*

T HE first half of the day's walk was through small suburban towns that are arrayed like pearls on a necklace in the El Bierzo Valley. I spent the first eight kilometers talking with Miguel from Teruel, Spain. This may not strike you, Dear Reader, as remarkable except for the fact that Miguel spoke no English. None. Zip. Nada. My Spanish must have improved because I was able to communicate a veritable wonderland of facts and receive responses that, with some effort and clarification, I generally understood. For example, I learned that Miguel recently retired after seventeen years working in Teruel's coal mines. When queried about the danger of his chosen occupation, he told me that León coal miners are at much greater risk because there is more gas in León's coal mines than those in Teruel for reasons neither he could explain nor I could understand. He has two daughters and a six-month old grandchild. He beamed like a schoolboy when telling me this—and I beamed right back at him. My excellent Spanish allowed me to inquire as to why rabbits do not nibble the thriving, unfenced gardens we passed as we talked. Because, he responded, rabbits live near the river, which was presumably some distance away. I learned the Spanish word for "stork," though I forgot it by the time we had our first coffee break. In any case I wondered if I might be ready to seriously consider taking up Spanish translation in retirement. Clients were, no doubt, eagerly awaiting my return from the Camino.

We ran into Anna and Trevor at our coffee break in Columbrianos. Johan, Ira, Kieran, and Steph turned up later in the day when it was adult beverage time.

The Bierzo Valley. Perhaps Heaven looks like this.

We couldn't get into Albergue Leo right away, so we found a grocery store and bought the ingredients for a delicious spaghetti and meatballs lunch, which we prepared in the *albergue's* kitchen. We were embarrassed by our ignorance of how the stove worked. One of us had to ask the *hospitalera* for assistance. She was very sweet, but I suspect that there may have been a thought bubble hovering over her head that read "Stupid men. Can't even boil water." A Korean pilgrim traded us our extra mushrooms for a delightful bowl of tasty watermelon. This was an excellent swap. We had a bowl of spaghetti left over that we gave to another Korean pilgrim who seemed very grateful indeed for this good fortune.

In days gone by, pilgrims too sick or exhausted to continue could go through this door near Villafranca del Bierzo and still receive an indulgence. I almost knocked on the door myself.

Albergue Leo was a delightful place. The *hospitalera*, Maria, was a very sweet lady, and a gracious host. Perhaps thirty-five years old, she ran the place with her recently widowed mother, Mercedes ("Like the car," she told me with a wink). When Maria asked me from the bottom of the stairs whether she would see us before we left the next morning, I told her it was unlikely, as we usually leave early. She ran up the stairs to give me a hug and one of those very proper kisses on both cheeks. It was touching.

My feet protested all morning, even though the distance was relatively short that day—only fifteen miles—and despite the lack of big hills. When I changed socks about eleven miles into the walk I discovered three new blisters which I named "Crap," "Darnit," and "Oh Fudge." Truth be told, Craig and I were red-hot annoyed with our feet. When we got to Villafranca we found a combination bike shop-chainsaw dealer-sporting goods store that had sandals in both our sizes. The place might have been named "Just What You Need, Just When You Need It." My feet felt such a sense of liberation as I crowbarred my trail runners off and slipped into the commodious environs of my new purchase. Freshly shod, would my cadaverous toes eventually recover? Only time would tell. Did the sight of Craig and

I walking about town in our matching sandals occasion comments from passersby? I could have cared less.

There was a married couple of sixtysomethings staying with us in Albergue Leo. We had seen them from time to time in various places. They were from the USA—Portland or Seattle, I think. I am sure I learned their names at some point, but I'm renaming them "The Louds." Mr. and Mrs. Loud could be heard speaking among themselves or to others as if they and all in their immediate orbit were hard of hearing. As I typed the notes for this entry in another room in a different section of the house, I could tell you how far they walked that day (thirty-ONE kilometers!), where they began (Campos!), what they had for lunch (sandwiches!), which parts of their feet were sore and blistered (left big toe for him! right little toe for her!), and a hundred additional intimacies normally whispered between spouses of a certain age. I vowed that if we reached La Faba the next day and they were there, I would sleep in the field with the cows.

We met a fellow in Albergue Leo who ended up sharing our bunkroom with us. Robbie was a wire-thin Aussie with a big, friendly personality—the kind of person who makes an instant connection with those with whom he comes into contact. Robbie had the appearance of a long-distance runner. He carried not an ounce of fat on his body, but he did carry the biggest backpack I had yet seen on the Camino. What's more, he also carried a smaller daypack on his chest. I cannot imagine what he had stashed in those two packs, but whatever it was, its weight didn't dampen his spirits a bit.

Craig and I headed off to Mass in our swanky new sandals. La Colegiata de Santa María del Cluniaco was one of several ancient churches in the town. Its origins were from the twelfth century, when it served as an important Cluniac outpost of pilgrim hospitality and spirituality. Most of the original building has been covered over by renovations that date back to the 1400s. The Mass was lovely, and a wonderful way to conclude our pilgriming for the day.

Our walk to La Faba the next day would only be about fifteen miles, but the last hour or so would be steeply uphill as we made our way to the top of the Camino's last really big mountain, which we'd crest when we arrive in O Cebreiro. As I prepared for bed, I reflected on my gratitude for how simple, uncluttered, and uncomplicated life becomes after three weeks of doing little else but walking, thinking, and praying.

Chapter 27

Villafranca del Bierzo to La Faba

Give to me, O Lord God, a stalwart heart,
which no tribulation can overcome.
— *Aquinas, Aquinas Prayer Book*

W E enjoyed our best sleep yet at Albergue Leo. Sleeping between two actual cotton sheets with a fluffy blanket in a room with only a few other people might not sound like much, but it is delightful. A pilgrim should be grateful for what he receives, and I was.

Our walk that day was quite delightful. We enjoyed the bright, clear skies to which we had become accustomed. The path was mostly alongside a lightly traveled road, except when it brought us up and through several small towns along the way. Eventually we reached Herrerias, as we knew we would, and we began to climb—first on pavement and then on rocks salted with plenty of road apples. It was not a long climb—perhaps thirty minutes—but when it topped out at La Faba, I had, as my five-year-old granddaughter Greta has been known to report, a "sweaty back."

We had reservations at one of the two *albergues* in the one-horse town that was La Faba, Spain. I was hoping to be able to stay at the *albergue* run by a German confraternity, Vltreia e.V., from Stuttgart, but it did not accept reservations, so to assure ourselves of beds for the night, I'd booked us at the other *albergue*. But we arrived early enough that we secured an advantaged place in line that allowed us admission to the place we preferred.

A church group from Manchester, England beat us to La Faba, but they weren't carrying packs. It worried me a bit to see tour groups this early on the Camino. But these were delightful folks who shared their bananas and apples with us. We enjoyed a friendly chat while sitting on the ancient wall that bordered the *albergue's* yard.

Craig hiked in his swanky new sandals all day, which really helped his ruined feet. I opted to continue wearing my shoes, and was grateful to peel them off after the walk with no new blisters noted.

The landscape was very Galician, even though we would not technically enter Galicia until just before O Cebreiro the next day. Still, green hills, brown cows, and Galician place names were becoming the norm as we inched our way closer and closer to the final autonomous province through which our pilgrimage would take us. I found myself loving it. Loving it very much indeed.

There was a couple with a small child—perhaps four months old—sharing the *albergue* with us. Mom carried Junior in a front pack and Dad lugged the gear. Their beds were not far from mine. I hoped that tyke was a good sleeper. He was wailing as I wrote my notes in preparation for this chapter, but he slept like a champ once put to bed for the evening.

While enjoying a late-afternoon beer at La Faba's lone cafe, Craig and I gave a loud "halooo" to Robbie as he and the world's biggest backpack rounded the corner. He had just come from the *albergue* where we were staying and complained that it was full. He was worried about having to continue hiking through this sparsely populated stretch of mountains to the next village in search of a bed. It was at that moment that I realized that I had failed to cancel my reservation at El Refugio, which sat just a few feet away across the street. "Robbie," I whispered, "I think I may be able to be of service. Wait here." I walked across the street, entered El Refugio's beaded entrance, and asked the *hospitalera* if she was still holding two beds for Craig and I. She told me that she was indeed. When I informed her that we would no longer require the beds, she bristled noticeably. "Why didn't you cancel?" she inquired saltily. "But that is precisely what I am doing at this very moment," I responded. She harrumphed a bit more as I beat a hasty retreat out the door to tell Robbie that there was now a bed available in La Faba. He was transformed into 150 pounds of Down Under smile.

There was an old chapel next to the *albergue*—Iglesia de San Andrés. It was a nice setting in which to offer my prayers that evening. There was an ecumenical prayer service run by the Stuttgart *hospilateros* in the chapel at 5:00. Pilgrims from various language groups were recruited to read scripture, while the service leader read a commentary in English. I recall with special fondness an Italian named Reynaldo. His emotions welled to the surface as he read his assigned text, and for the rest of the service he sat quietly and wept. It was a touching moment.

We passed the one hundred-mile mark during the day's walk, and predicted that we would be in Santiago in ninety-six miles. I was so eager to get there and to see Carol again. We would be reuniting in Santiago almost exactly forty years after we were married. Forty years of anything is a long time, and forty years of marriage lends itself to a kind of "code-talk of the heart" that is difficult to describe to those who have not experienced it.

Chapter 28

La Faba to Triacastela

Give to me, O Lord God, a temperate heart,
which no violent passion can enslave.
—Aquinas, Aquinas Prayer Book

W E entered Galicia on a steep mountain path under brightening skies framed by peaks of stunning beauty. But the climb from La Faba to O Cebreiro was an ass-kicker. The path wound steadily upward around the shoulders of tall mountains. It was dark when we began the climb, but the sun eventually poked its face above the eastern horizon and lit the way as we stepped out of Castilla y León, into Galicia, and ever upward toward O Cebreiro.

Two enter Galicia.

There were so many stunning vistas as we made our way through the mountains that they were difficult to quantify. The hillsides were covered with gorse and heather in brilliant bloom. As we climbed higher we were able to look down upon mist-filled valleys with their hidden mysteries that would not be revealed until the sun rose higher to burn the fog away. Each part of the Camino is filled with a different kind of natural beauty, but the mountains of Galicia have a particular charm that romantic verse of starry-eyed poets.

We walked for a bit between Fonfria and Triacastela with a retired Australian cop whose name I failed to record. He was a tall, fit fellow with a booming voice and a confident stride—the kind of person who never met a stranger. He carried the conversation with little assistance from me. He informed us that someone took his and other pilgrims' money, credit cards, passports, phones, and other valuables from the *albergue* in O Cebreiro. The thief posed as a pilgrim and rifled his victims' backpacks as they got up in the middle of the night to use the bathroom. The police were called, but did not seem too interested in an aggressive investigation. This was so disappointing. I will confess to developing a naive trust of all with whom I engaged while on pilgrimage. And while I never encountered a single problem in 1,000 miles of walking across Spain, it was also a good reminder to keep our valuables close at all times. Crime on the Camino is not unknown, but it is rare.

A thatch-roofed *palloza* of O Cebreiro. (SanchoPanzaXXI,
CC BY-SA 3.0, via Wikimedia Commons)

The sixteen miles we walked between La Faba and Triacastela felt much longer because of the hills and the blisters that seemed to bloom on my feet like dandelions in spring. This pilgrimage was definitely harder on my feet than the first time I walked the Camino in 2016. But there was little to do but tape 'em up and walk again the next day. A pilgrim must suffer, I guess.

Our pilgrimage coincided with election season. From time to time we passed posters advertising the virtues of various political candidates vying for the privilege of public office. Most posters depicted images of smiling politicians whose confident visage conveyed public-minded vocations eager for leadership. Which is why I chuckled when we came upon a campaign poster for the mayor of Samos, Julio Gallego Moure. The son of former mayor Julio Gallego Losada, Mayor Moure's campaign poster depicted a man completely unconcerned about his prospects for reelection. He had served as mayor since 2007, and had been elected three times since. His campaign poster might as well have said "You know you're going to vote for me. I'm your mayor for life. I dare you to vote for anyone else."[1]

Samos's mayor in his best election suit.

1. Spanish politics have a long history of cronyism, shenanigans, and back-room deals that any ward boss in Chicago or Boston would recognize. When an election official from Granada arrived at the local men's club (or *Casino*) to announce the results in a late-nineteenth-century plebiscite, he reported the following: "We the Liberals were convinced that we would win these elections. However, the will of God has decreed otherwise. It appears that we the Conservatives have won the elections" (Preston, *People Betrayed,* 27).

Our *albergue* in Triacastela—Complexo Xacobeo—was nice. We shared it, and the town, with many familiar faces. Mr. and Mrs. Loud were present and accounted for, and filled us in on all the news there was to shout. A group of Southwest Baptist University students rolled into the *albergue*, tired and footsore but happy. We ate dinner with three ladies from Seattle—Eileen, Dawn, and Beth. We had seen these gals from time to time over the past couple of weeks. They were definite S & B material.[2] They pilgrimed in style, staying in hotels and having their packs transported. Eileen and Dawn were thoroughly enjoying the experience, but Beth, well, she was gritting her teeth, praying for the end of the trail. Eileen and Dawn frequently rolled their eyes in her direction.

The next day we would walk through Sarria, where we expected an already busy Camino to get even busier since pilgrims can walk from Sarria and still obtain their *compostela* certificate in Santiago. We booked beds in all the towns we would stay in for the rest of the pilgrimage to avoid the stress of racing others for a place to sleep.

Along the path near Alto do Poio we ran into a family of Danes. Mom and Dad were walking with a thirteen-year-old girl and a ten-year-old boy. It was a very touching scene to observe Mom and Dad strolling along The Way chatting comfortably about this or that while their youngsters ran ahead to explore the various wonders along the path. This encounter made me miss my family even more.

2 See p. 3.

Chapter 29

Triacastela to Barbadelo

Give to me, O Lord my God, understanding of You, diligence in seeking You, wisdom in finding You, discourse ever pleasing to You, perseverance in waiting for You, and confidence in finally embracing You.
—Aquinas, Aquinas Prayer Book

W ORDS I never imagined writing while on pilgrimage include "I had a lovely afternoon sitting next to the crystal, cooling waters of the *albergue's* luxurious swimming pool." And yet, there I was tapping the keys of my phone, writing those exact words. When Joe and I ducked into the Casa Barbadelo on a gray afternoon in 2016—an afternoon that promised and delivered rain—I remember thinking "I bet that pool would be pleasant if the weather cooperated." Well, three years later it cooperated. How that place pays its bills by charging penny-pinching pilgrims €10 each is beyond my understanding. Still, I was glad to be there after a relatively short fourteen-miler from Triacastela.

Barbadelo has a checkered medieval past. David Gitlitz and Linda Kay Davidson explain that in the twelfth century unscrupulous innkeepers from Santiago de Compostela traveled as far as Barbadelo and Triacastela to trick unsuspecting pilgrims into parting with their cash by means of nefarious offers of Christian hospitality once they reached St. James's city.

They would provide the pilgrims with a token that the pilgrims should present upon arrival, whereupon "my wife and family will provide well for you out of love for me." The pilgrims—no doubt deeply grateful for such gospel-motivated kindness—would arrive in Santiago, be seated at table, and then sold candles at a marked up rate to be lit when visiting the shrine containing the saint's relics.[1] We were grateful to be treated with a more authentic and transparent hospitality.

Finding an *albergue* with a four-star swimming pool on a hot day in the middle of Nowhere, Spain after a fourteen-mile hike is improbable. Being introduced to a fellow pilgrim who is a friend of someone you know back in your hometown is a minor miracle. But that is just what happened. While soaking my blistered feet and sore muscles in the cooling waters of Casa Barbadelo's pool I greeted a man about my age who was doing likewise. He responded in American English, and we eventually got around to asking each other where we were from. When I told him I was from Holland, Michigan he responded that he had a friend there—Russ Richardson.

"The same Russ Richardson I have coffee with from time to time?" I asked, slackjawed.

"Yeah, I guess so," he responded.

"Tall guy? Close cropped hair? Former Camino pilgrim?"

Well, I'll be darned. It turns out that Matt and his wife Barbie have walked thousands of miles on various Camino routes—many of them with Russ. Small world? I'd say so.

By the time we got past O Cebreiro there were fewer mountains, but there were many steep climbs and descents to and from numerous rivers. Every day was a "sweaty back" day. And the temperatures were definitely climbing. Our walk from Triacastela to Barbadelo topped out at 85° F.

Galicia was so beautiful. The photos I shared with my family at the end of each day were entirely inadequate. The ageless chestnut trees—twisted with the years and sprouting branches willy-nilly—crowned both sides of the sunken paths providing shady views of adjacent pastures enclosed by stone walls that seem to be from Old Testament times. If it wasn't so damned hard I'd be a professional walker in a place like this.

1. Gitlitz and Davidson, *Pilgrimage Road to Santiago*, 318–19.

Welcome to Galicia! (Jeff Vanuga, Public domain, via Wikimedia Commons)

The rural Galicia we were traversing was Green Acres on steroids. Cows, chickens, pigs, and lazy farm dogs regarded us with gimlet eye as we walked through their realm. The background aroma could best be described as "good country air." But this is simply a polite way of saying that everything smelled like cow shit. After awhile we simply grew accustomed to the reek. That is, until we exited Sarria. Perhaps two miles after leaving Sarria's paved environs we were back walking among farm fields. One farmer was fertilizing his field with a tractor-drawn trailer lavishly spraying liquid manure fifty yards behind and to either side of his tractor. The smell was so overpoweringly cloying that Craig and I literally gagged our way along the Camino with eyes watering and our picnic lunch threatening to reemerge, and forcefully so. In 2016, John Thomson, Alison Craighead, and Euan McCall concocted a perfume that contained each substance referenced in the *Book of Revelation*.[2] A touch of brimstone, a dash of sulfur, etc, etc. All they really needed to do was stroll past that farmer's field for a whiff of hell. But let us give Galician farmers credit where credit is due. Manure as fertilizer is a much more sustainable, affordable, and ecologically prudent approach than the use of commercially produced anhydrous ammonia, superphosphate, and muriate of potash.[3] Manure is what they have on hand, and combined with the copious rainfall of that terrifically green place, nobody should ever grow hungry there.

Craig finally threw his boots away. It was all sandals all the time for him from Barbadelo forward. The $3 Detroit Tigers flip-flops that had

---

2. *BBC World Update*, "What Does Hell Smell Like?"

3. Logsdon, *Holy Shit*, 5.

accompanied me through nearly 1,000 miles of Spain gave up the ghost a couple of days earlier.

I talked with a seventy-five-year-old fellow for awhile while walking between San Xil and Furela. I first met Reynaldo at the ecumenical prayer service in La Faba. He was an Italian from Milan. He spoke no English. Neither did Reynaldo speak Spanish. My Italian is limited to "spaghetti" and "Sophia Loren." Still we enjoyed a delightful hour of hand gestures, Twenty Questions, Charades, and Google Translate. It was fun.

The students from Southwest Baptist University arrived at Casa Barbadelo after we had settled in. They could not have been more surprised to learn that I had been to their university for a consulting gig some years before. They were nice kids, but were limping badly since they had only recently begun the Camino and did not have their walking legs just yet.

The gratitude I felt for the undeserved grace in my life was settling deep in my bones by this point in the pilgrimage. The anger from which I sought healing three years previous was gone. In its place I was fortunate to have a renewed sense of vocation and forward-looking optimism. The long walks and empty miles of the Camino were proving to be an excellent place to acknowledge how fortunate I was, for it was not necessarily fore-ordained that things would turn out as they had in my life. Family, friends, and the grace of a loving God all conspired in a marvelous way to pull me from the angry depths in which I was seemingly stuck, just like Christian wallowing in the Slough of Despond in Bunyan's tale.[4]

4. Bunyan, *Pilgrim's Progress*, 5.

Chapter 30

Barbadelo to Castromayor

Grant that with Your hardships I may be burdened in reparation here, that Your benefits I may use in gratitude upon the way, that in Your joys I may delight by glorifying You in the Kingdom of Heaven.
— Aquinas, Aquinas Prayer Book

WE had a long day—more than eighteen miles—and the weather had turned hot. I ran out of water about five kilometers before we reached our *albergue* in Castromayor, and I was wobbly by the time we arrived. I have never been more grateful to shower and rehydrate.

I mentioned earlier in this memoir that mile-counting is a bad idea while on pilgrimage. But from time to time one simply cannot help taking note of significant milestones. We had one of those shortly after leaving Barbadelo. As the sun rose in the morning sky we came upon the 100-kilometer marker. Knowing that we were only sixtyish miles from Santiago— and mere days away from being reunited with our sweethearts—buoyed our spirits considerably.

The "towns" through which we walked on this stretch of the Camino were little more than dots on the map. Seemingly abandoned, they appeared to be farms without farmers, buildings without occupants, shops without customers, streets without vehicles, and places without people. Most of the pilgrimage to St. James is through empty countryside. One looks forward to occasional interludes of civilization. I will confess to wondering if we had walked into a dystopian novel when we encountered—well, when we *didn't* encounter—anyone in village after Galician village. It was a bit spooky, though not for long. As soon as we said "Here we are" we would follow up with "There we go." In fact, the farmers in this part of Spain live in small hamlets—though they show up on the map as towns—of only a few houses. Many of the houses are divided in such a way that the farm animals live downstairs and the family upstairs.[1]

We stopped for coffee, a light breakfast, and groceries for lunch in Portomarín. This Galician town is interesting for several reasons. Situated on the Miño River, it was completely relocated to its present location when the river was dammed as a flood control/hydroelectric power project. The ancient Iglesia de San Juan was reconstructed—stone by stone—as part of the town's relocation. Another bit of fascinating trivia about Portomarín is that the Camino directs pilgrims over the river, into the town, and then takes them *back over the river* via a different bridge before continuing westward toward Santiago de Compostela. Hot, weary pilgrims the world over grumble about the excessive mileage.

One of the more delightful aspects of our walk in this section of the Camino was the company of Araceli and Raechel—both young physical therapists who joined our "pilgrim bubble" in Boadilla. Both had recently finished their professional education and were considering their options for how to launch their careers. They were light-hearted, engaging, and helped us grandfathers maintain a younger vibe as we pilgrimed along The Way.

Araceli and Raechel

1. Gitlitz and Davidson, *Pilgrimage Road to Santiago,* 318.

The last twelve kilometers of the walk from Portomarín to Castromayor were gradually but steadily uphill. It was very hot. Near Gonzar we passed a woman who was walking very slowly, and by all appearances was in some distress. We slowed our pace—which was already slow—and inquired about her welfare. She did not speak English, and it was not obvious to me which language she responded to our questions with. In any case, she conveyed through hand gestures and facial expressions that she would be OK, and so we walked on. Fifteen minutes later we came to a shaded grove and encountered a group of English-speaking pilgrims. We mentioned our concerns about the lady laboring along the path behind us and asked the men resting against the stone wall to give her an orange we fished out of Craig's pack. They readily agreed, for which we were grateful. We were hot, tired, and thirsty, and she appeared to be considerably worse off than us.

We shared Albergue Ortiz with the SBU students, Marianne from Germany (whom we had traveled alongside for a week or two), and Araceli and Raechel. Castromayor seemed to have one thing—the *albergue* we stayed in. Just a few barns and crowing roosters besides that. It was 90°F in the bunkroom, making sleep difficult and uncomfortable. Fate was evening things out after our luxurious afternoon at the swimming pool in Barbadelo.

Chapter 31

Castromayor[1] to Melidè

Let me cling to nothing, save only to you.
— *Aquinas, Aquinas Prayer Book*

W E had been walking for more than one month, and finally marked the first day of June as we arose at 4:00 am. We wanted to get as much of our nearly twenty miles in that day before the heat grew too severe. Araceli and Raechel joined us and were on the path by 4:20. It was a good thing that Craig and Araceli had headlamps, because the one I bought in Carrión to replace the one I brought from home did not work. I had bad luck with headlamps on this Camino.

The Milky Way—the *Via Lactea*—shone bright over the Camino as we left Castromayor. (Photo by Denis Degioanni on Unsplash)

1. This village is spelled either "Castromayor" or "Castromaior," depending on the publication.

The stars were brilliant that morning. Perhaps twenty minutes after leaving the *albergue* we stopped, turned off the headlamps, and simply stared up at the Milky Way as it pointed us toward Santiago de Compostela.

The Camino was growing more crowded with both end-to-end pilgrims and tour groups carrying small daypacks walking only the last bit to Santiago. I tried to not be too grumpy about it. I did not have any right to complain. There was even some benefit to sharing The Way with the day-trippers. We would run into each other in the cafes and bars and they would pepper us with questions, in obvious awe of our evident superhero stamina in walking all the way from France, carrying all that we needed on our backs. They made us feel like bulletproof Olympians.

As part of my morning devotions each day I read and reflected on a note I received from Dynamic Catholic. This ministry had been helpful to me in framing the gospel in useful, practical ways. Imagine my surprise as we walked along that morning and, as I looked to my left, I saw a Dynamic Catholic bus parked in the field next to the Camino path. I told Craig, Araceli, and Raechel that I would catch up with them at the next coffee stop and I went over for a chat with the Dynamic Catholic pilgrims. Unfortunately, the bus was empty, save for the driver, who could not have been more pleasant. I told him about my esteem for Dynamic Catholic's ministry and he offered me my pick from a box filled with tasty snacks. *Muchisimas gracias Sr. conductor de autobús!* When I reconnected with Craig, Araceli,

and Raechel at the next cafe it was filled with the Dynamic Catholic pilgrims. We had a very nice chat. Did I mention that they thought we had superpowers?

Each Galician farm has a traditional *horreo* to keep the mice out of the seed corn. This one is shared by the entire village. (Luis Miguel Bugallo Sánchez (Lmbuga), CC BY-SA 4.0, via Wikimedia Commons)

It was another warm day, with temperatures that eventually rose to the mid-eighties. Just as we had the day before, we walked past an older pilgrim who labored badly as he shuffled up the path at a snail's pace. We stopped to check on him, but he insisted that he was fit enough to continue without assistance. But I am telling you, he looked like Walking Death. He had some food and enough water so we said a little prayer for him and walked on.

We passed through a number of seemingly abandoned villages during the early morning. None offered any services at such an hour. After approximately fifteen kilometers we reached Palas de Rei—population 3,743. It was there that Raechel realized that she had left her *credencial* and journal in the Castromayor *albergue*. Araceli—fluent in Spanish—called the *albergue* but the hosts had not seen these precious documents. Raechel was understandably heartbroken because she would need her pilgrim passport to get her *compostela* at the cathedral in Santiago. But Fortune would smile on her pilgrimage that day. Craig and I ran into the SBU students on the street in Melidè, and they said that one in their group had the documents. They promised to bring them to us, and we brought them to Raechel later that evening. Joy and thanksgiving ensued.

La Parroquia de San Tirso in Palas de Rei, where Raechel's documents were found to be missing. (Calimerojoseluis, CC BY-SA 3.0 ES, via Wikimedia Commons)

We arrived in Melidè around 12:30 and checked into the Albergue Cruceiro. Luis showed us up to our second-story room. We were the first to arrive and so had our pick of the beds. Since it was so warm we picked the beds closest to the window. This would turn out to be a strategic error, for the *albergue's* first floor was a bar and our room was right above it. The patrons hooted and hollered the night away as we laid staring at the ceiling, waiting for the blessed relief of dawn.

Late in the afternoon the fellow I mentioned earlier—the slowster whom we feared might see his final day on the Camino—staggered into our room. Dieter was from Germany. He lived near Koblenz which is the town my great (great-great?) grandfather immigrated from, avoiding conscription in the Kaiser's army. Dieter had a lung problem of indeterminate diagnosis and prognosis that forced him to walk very slowly. Yet, there he was. I hoped I would be able to sleep that night with Dieter's nonstop, gurgling cough. As it turned out, the bar patrons on the sidewalk below drowned him out almost completely. Ugh.

Melidè is famous for restaurants that serve *Pulpo a la Gallega*—octopus Galician style. We thought we might treat ourselves to this delicacy at dinner, but first we had to figure out what to eat for lunch. Craig was sick of sandwiches, so we bought frozen croquettes at the grocery store and cooked them in the *albergue's* kitchen. Well, we did not have enough oil to properly pan fry them, so they turned out a bit burned and mushy. We ate them anyway. And our dreams of *pulpo* for dinner never materialized. The people we were with wanted hamburgers, so we went with the crowd. We decided we would wait until Dar and Carol arrived so we could enjoy *pulpo* together. Fat chance.

I could hardly believe that there were only two more days to walk. It was a good thing though, because my feet probably did not have much more than two days left to give. The next day's walk would require us to meander twenty-one miles from Melidè to Arca/Pedrouzo/Pino. And it was predicted to be another scorcher, so we set the alarm for another 4:00 am start.

Chapter 32

Melidè to Arca/Pedrouzo/Pino

With thanksgiving let me remember, O my God, all your mercies to me and let me confess them to you. Let my bones be filled with your love.

—St. Augustine of Hippo[1]

ANOTHER hot day of weather was predicted as the cooling breezes of spring gave up the ghost to the Front Porch of Hell that is the Spanish summer. I would like to say that our alarm woke us up at 4:00 to get an early start on the day, but one cannot "awake" if one has not "slept." While lying in our beds through the night, fully conscious, we received a free education in the differences between "Spanish" and "Loud Drunk Spanish" as the patrons at the bar whooped it up outside our window. Did you know that scientific studies have definitively demonstrated that alcohol consumption actually decreases a partygoer's hearing?[2] It's true, and seems to be a bigger problem for men than for women. The effect, of course, is that the more one drinks, the louder one speaks, lest one's interlocutors fail to understand one's every word. Any doubts I may have had about the veracity of this claim were erased utterly on that sultry night in Melidè.

1. Augustine, *Confessions*, 143.
2. Upile et al., "Acute Effects."

We had planned to walk to Pedrouzo with Araceli and Raechel. They made the wise choice to stay in Albergue San Antón on the quiet street of the same name. Craig and I crept through the darkened streets of Melidè to meet them outside of their lodgings. We were a few minutes early, so we waited patiently while nibbling bananas. Four-thirty—our appointed rendezvous time—came and went. The *albergue* windows were dark. At 4:35 we perceived a rustling behind the front door. Hushed voices whispered inquiries to each other.

"How do we get out? Can you find the lock? You can't?! Oh, you can, but it won't open? Let's try the back door."

More patient waiting ensued. The street was as quiet as the grave. We expected Araceli and Raechel to walk around the corner of the building at any moment. Time slowed to a crawl, then seemed to stop altogether. After twenty minutes we concluded that the ladies were locked inside the *albergue*—just as Craig and I found ourselves incarcerated at the *albergue* in Espinal on the third day of our pilgrimage. Though we felt bad about it, we decided to leave without Araceli and Raechel, hoping that they might catch up to us once they broke out of jail.

I wish I could have typed "Today was a mountaintop experience unmatched in the history of pilgrimage." But that would be pure prevarication. The walk that day was uneventful. Vanilla. Perhaps the most noteworthy event involved getting lost. It was still very early in the morning—and black as midnight—when I turned to Craig and said "Say, by any chance have you seen a yellow arrow anytime in, let's say, the last thirty minutes?"

"Yellow arrow? Hmm, by golly, I don't believe I have!" Craig responded in a voice tinged with wonderment and surprise as if yellow arrows were a novelty with which we were unaccustomed.

We kept walking but began to shine Craig's headlamp on every possible surface to see if we could spot a *flecha amarilla*. No dice.

"Let's split up, look for an arrow, and meet back here in five minutes," I suggested.

The next thing I knew I was wandering around in the backyard of a farmhouse, waking up the crowing roosters and barking dogs and generally raising a ruckus. Five minutes later we reconnected and admitted that we were lost, in the middle of nowhere, in the dark, and one of us did not have a headlamp. We did the only thing we could do—we turned around and started walking back from whence we came. You are no doubt sitting on your couch in your favorite room sipping a refreshing beverage and asking yourself "What's the big deal?" But what you must try to understand is that no pilgrim voluntarily walks back. Only forward. Toward the goal. This event could be titled "Our Collective Shame." Still, we had little choice. Twenty minutes later we came to a crossroads and spotted the yellow arrow we had missed. How did we miss it? Inattention? Slothful pilgriming? Original sin? Who knows? We turned left, and those who were once lost were now found, and prodigal no more.

Keep your eyes open—especially in the dark. (Photo by Jon Tyson on Unsplash)

As we approached Arzúa we ran into three students from Thomas More College of the Liberal Arts. This town was the only population center of any import we encountered before arriving in Pedrouzo. The students were theology majors, and proved to be interesting conversation partners as we strolled through that center of Galician cheesemaking.

We arrived at the day's destination in the early afternoon. We could not be blamed if we had kept walking right through the town, unaware that we had, in fact, arrived. That town—for reasons passing understanding—goes by one of three names: Arca, O Pedrouzo, and O Pino. Each name seems to be in common use. There was official signage at various crossroads with each name. Cross one street and you would be sure you were in O Pino. Walk another block and you would be convinced that you had crossed some sort of invisible municipal border and were now in O Pedrouzo. Five minutes later and you might say to yourself "Arca? Huh?" It's not like the denizens of that place say "I live in Arca, which in the old days was called O Pino." Or "O Pedrouzo is where I live, but send the check to me in Arca." If one Googles any of the three placenames the search will return the same dot on the map. This seems like an unwise system, sure to engender confusion. It would be like calling the largest city in the United States Gotham, The Big Apple, or New York City interchangeably and officially. Perhaps the triple-named characteristic of this town of more than 6,000 souls is occasioned by the fact that there are two official languages there—Spanish and Galician (or *gallego*). What accounts for the third version is a Camino mystery.

At Coffee Break Number Two in Salceda, Craig and I were chatting with a British lady when I noticed a motorcycle cop ride past at speed. Two minutes later five more flew past. A few minutes after that ten more rode by, the thunder of their bikes splitting the peace and tranquility of the Galician countryside. At this point we wondered what was happening down the road in the direction of all this law enforcement. No sooner had we exited the cafe when thirty, forty, or perhaps even fifty more mounted police screamed past, heading somewhere in a big hurry. Nobody we asked knew why. The world's biggest car accident? A convention of motorcycle police? It was a mystery. Backpacks donned, we pointed ourselves west and kept walking. After perhaps thirty minutes the mystery was solved as dozens and dozens of cyclists rode past. The police were serving as security for this road race at all the intersections for the next twenty miles.

These guys provided a welcome diversion on an otherwise vanilla day.
(Photo by Markus Spiske on Unsplash)

After checking in at the Albergue Porta de Santiago we went through our usual arrival routine, which always included showering, laundering our clothing, and a brief nap. But our minds were already focused on Santiago and, after that, a reunion with Carol and Dar. Once they arrived in a few days we would enjoy a ten-day vacation together. After a few days in Santiago de Compostela we would go to San Sebastian, and then conclude our trip in Barcelona for the final days of our post-pilgrimage vacation. We needed to book train tickets from Santiago to San Sebastian, and I was having a hard time doing this on my phone. The *hospitalero* directed us to a hotel down the street that had a computer we could use. We found the hotel, fed some coins into the device that granted us access, and then had an interesting experience navigating the *Renfe* (Spanish National Railway) website in Spanish, as I could not pull up the English version. Four train ticket bookings later, we decided we had earned a beer. Perhaps two beers.

Not every town in which we stayed had an evening Mass, but Arca/Pedrouzo/Pino did. As we walked through the town toward Iglesia Santa Eulalia Del Arca Pedrouzo we were joined—one by one and two by two—by other pilgrims eager to worship on the last evening of their pilgrimage. Three things impressed me about this Mass. First, the pilgrims and the townsfolk mingled casually and comfortably on the plaza in front of the church while waiting for the church to open. It was nice. I had been to many Masses in Spain, and it was more common for pilgrims and locals to keep to themselves. Iglesia Santa Eulalia Del Arca Pedrouzo was a pleasant change. Second, the sanctuary had a very interesting scallop shell motif for its retablo. The scallop shell is, of course, ubiquitous along the Camino. It is incorporated into various architectural elements of buildings sacred and secular from Paris to Finisterre. But the church in Pedrouzo was the first I had seen to have this iconic design so intimately integrated with the principal object of religious devotion—the tabernacle. Finally, the priest was an interesting aspect of this Mass. The Mass began as usual—in Spanish as I expected. But then the prayers struck my ears differently. What language had he switched to? Italian! And then to English! During the homily he explained that he was an Italian priest assigned to Arca by his order for a couple of years. He was full of good cheer and encouraged us pilgrims as we neared the conclusion of our pilgrimage.

Iglesia Santa Eulalia Del Arca Pedrouzo and its scallop shell retablo.
(Simona C via Foursquare)

The next day was to be our most significant yet—arrival in Santiago de Compostela. As I laid in my bunk, the memories of the last month came flooding through my mind like a swift-flowing stream in springtime. We had had so many meaningful experiences. We had met so many terrific, inspiring people. I understood my life differently as a result of a long walk over a long time.

Chapter 33

Arca/Pedrouzo/Pino to Santiago de Compostela

"In all created things discern the providence and wisdom of God, and in all things give Him thanks."

— ST. TERESA OF AVILA[1]

O UR desires are—or should be—the object of perpetual reassessment as we pilgrim through this life. Our desires are shimmering shapeshifters, first appearing one way and then morphing into something seemingly different—like an image in a funhouse mirror. When we are children we desire adulthood. As hormone-charged teenagers we desire a lover and marriage. When we are part of the workaday proletariat we desire the leisure of the weekend, and then of retirement. Old and infirm, we desire to turn back the clock to days of vigor and independence. Our desires can fool us, and ought to be interrogated for the imposters they can sometimes appear to be.

Pilgrims to St. James cannot help desiring the end of The Way—to walk into the Praza de Obradoiro, and lift their eyes to the wonders of the cathedral and what lies within. And yet, a creeping sense of loss marks

1. Lovasik, *Catholic prayer*, 81.

the final days of the pilgrimage. "It's coming to an end," we sigh, as our minds slowly but inexorably begin to grip the realities that await us in the nonpilgrim world to which we are about to return. We sigh for the loss of the pilgrim's road, even if our longing for loved ones from which the pilgrimage has separated us is a physical ache.

And so it was for Craig and me as we awoke to gray skies and wet pavements for our last day of walking. It was to be an all-day rain—the kind Galicians have come to regard as normal in their green, Celtic kingdom. It was the kind of day when a pilgrim's excitement for the arrival was tinged with regret for the ending—clothed first by rain jacket and covered by umbrella, only to eventually give in to the unrelenting fact of the rain and its utter inescapability. We would be wet that day, but only all day and everywhere.

We walked for awhile that day with Klaus, whom we had previously met on our walk into Burgos. He was a cheerful fellow whose company we enjoyed very much. Like us, he looked forward to the end of the pilgrimage and to being reunited with his wife in Bavaria. As we discussed various subjects, I regretted my inability to converse with Klaus in his native tongue. His English was entirely competent, though he searched for the right word in English from time to time. It felt like an inhospitable act to speak only in my language and not in his. But he was very kind, and I was grateful for his company.

Our walk that day was not very far—only about thirteen miles. But the weather and the psychic contrasts between "Let's get there!" and "Must it end?" made the morning drag by, with each mile seeming like two. We stopped for breakfast at a popular spot along the main road before the night formally transitioned to day. There were a host of pilgrims who had the same idea, and the place was a veritable Babel of languages from every corner of the world. The cafe staff seemed a bit wearied by it all, and not quite ready for the horde making its way toward Santiago.

The hill known as Monte de Gozo—Mount Joy—is an eagerly anticipated milestone on the pilgrim's last day. A mere five kilometers from Santiago, one looks forward to the first glimpse of the cathedral's towering spires from a point near the monument to Pope St. John Paul II's pilgrimages to St. James in the 1980s.[2] But there was no joy on that hilltop for Craig

2. In fact, Pope St. John Paul II made the pilgrimage to Santiago de Compostela twice during his pontificate—in 1982 and again in 1989 to observe World Youth Day. His message in 1989: "Santiago de Compostela is not only a sanctuary but also a way, that is, a dense net of itineraries for the pilgrims. The Way to Santiago has been a way of

and I as the rain fell in slanted sheets and mist concealed the approaches to the city. There was one consolation, however. Once the peak of Monte de Gozo has been crested, there are no more hills to climb. All of the "up" is behind, with nothing but blessed level ground from that point forward. Alleluia.

Pope Benedict XVI and Pope St. John Paul II, pilgrims to St. James.(José Luiz Bernardes Ribeiro, CC BY-SA 3.0 Via Wikimqedia Commons)

Santiago de Compostela is a reasonably large city with nearly 100,000 residents. Its old city is surrounded by a string of suburbs, including Lavacolla, San Marcos, and San Lázaro. Days and days of quiet paths and sleepy villages stand in sharp contrast to the sudden reintroduction to rushing traffic, roadside billboards, and multistory buildings. It was a bit dizzying.

The graffitied entrance to the city has seen better days.
(Simon Burchell, CC BY-SA 4.0, via Wikimedia Commons)

conversion and extraordinary testimony of faith for centuries." (John Paul II, "*Message of the Holy Father*," 3).

When a pilgrim walks through the *meseta* or along Galician farm roads he takes little notice nor cares very much for his appearance or grooming. But when he nears the end of the journey, with the prospect of seeing his sweetheart after a very long time, well, he wants to impress. And so it was for Craig and I as we negotiated Santiago's sodden outskirts and found a lonely barber with no customers. For a reasonable price Juan Carlos Esparis Agra transformed us from slovenly, unkempt hobos into respectable gentlemen of the world. With freshly coiffed hair and neatly trimmed chin whiskers we were ready for the last kilometers of the long, long road.

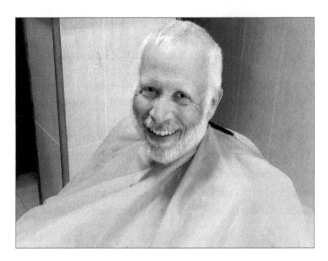

Former hobo.

The arrival was emotional for Craig. I too was impacted—and profoundly so. Art critic Eleanor Munro has described the arrival experience in a way I could certainly relate to:[3]

> . . . and then at last the road turns up a hill and around a corner and under an archway through a narrow passage right out into the square before the cathedral, where bagpipes are wheezing and drums are rattling and travelers shouting. Every pilgrimage place has such a collecting pool for new arrivals, where the very air seems tilted by the settling of pavement over centuries, and sounds are confused with echoes off buildings around the edges. So you are disoriented for a moment, even dizzy. And in this case,

3. Munro, *On Glory Roads*, 221–22.

it is necessary to walk a little further on to turn around to face the cathedral.

And then you are wiped out by the sight.

The Baroque facade, spouting purple-tinged, wind-seeded vines like seaweed, mounts like breakers, with pilasters and columns leaping upward, each one pulling the eyes up till they reach the froth of bell towers; and then begins the eyes' flight around the profile of the stones, up pyramids, domes, and pinnacles and over little urns and then up again to the towers where the topmost spires, like frozen droplets, fall upward into the sea of the sky . . .

And then you are wiped out by the sight. (Photo by rafael furtado on Unsplash)

We did not linger long in the plaza—just long enough to take the obligatory arrival photos. We went to the pilgrim office to see if we could get our *compostela*, but the line looked to be about two hours long. Given our soaked, cold state we thought that finding the hostel might be the best decision. The lady in the pilgrim office showed us the street on the map where our accommodation was located, but it was still difficult to find. The "street" turned out to be more of an "alley." The hostel was on the third floor of a nondescript gray building with little marking. But we were buzzed in, made our way upstairs and were warmly welcomed. The room was nice, had a private bathroom, and had beds without ladders. Perfect.

We went in search of lunch after showering and hanging clothes to dry from every possible hook, ledge, and vantage point the room had to offer. Craig's eagle eye spotted a traditional Galician restaurant on the way to the hostel: Burger King. I had the biggest, greasiest hamburger of my likely-to-be-shortened life. It came with an egg on it, and was just what the doctor ordered after thirty-two days of pilgrim fare.

Our need for American junk food satisfied, we went back to the pilgrim office and waited for about ninety minutes to get our *compostelas*. It was fun talking with others waiting in line, hearing their stories, and sharing ours.

We met a group of Camino friends for dinner after concluding our business in the Pilgrim Office. Harold, Ira, Stephanie, Nigel, Trevor, Anna, and a couple of tag-a-longs comprised the party. We ate at a funky place on the Rua de Franco. Everyone got a hug and a promise to stay in touch as the party broke up.

Afterword

WHEN does a pilgrim stop being a pilgrim and start being something else? In the case of the Camino de Santiago, is it when the pilgrim walks into the square in front of the cathedral? Does s/he walk into the Praza do Obradoiro as a pilgrim and out as a tourist? Or is it after the traditional pilgrim Mass? After the final blessing does the pilgrim take on a new label? Maybe the journey is still a pilgrimage until the pilgrim kneels and offers prayers of thanksgiving before the silver casket containing the relics of St. James in the cathedral crypt. Perhaps s/he kneels down as a pilgrim and rises as a tourist or mere traveler.

The Christian believer's life is brimming with pilgrimage heritage. Abraham, Moses and the escaping Israelites, Jesus and his apostles, and saints through the ages have all been pilgrims who have walked sacred journeys, to sacred places, for sacred purposes. And we believe that the present life is simply such a journey to another place. We are pilgrims on this earth, just passing through. Not meant to be here. Eager for what's better.

When does a pilgrim stop being a pilgrim? Perhaps we transition gradually, one step at a time. Perhaps we transition from the pilgrim state once our daily thoughts and actions unconsciously morph from pilgrim thoughts and actions to those of the world of which we are a part. If this is the case, may I never stop being a pilgrim. Never.

The day after our arrival we met Araceli and Raechel for breakfast. Poor Araceli was just beginning to recover from twenty-four hours of diarrhea and dehydration. She was able to take some orange juice and a bit of toast, but still looked pretty wrung out. Just like the night before with our other pilgrim pals, we traded hugs, best wishes, and promises to stay in touch.

Because the cathedral was undergoing extensive renovations, the pilgrim Mass was held in the nearby Iglesia de San Francisco. Before the Mass began, we went back to the sacristy and were given a certificate from the Franciscan confraternity attesting to our pilgrimage and visit to this important church dedicated to St. Francis of Assisi—himself a pilgrim to Santiago de Compostela.

I went to confession before Mass and was shriven by a kind Franciscan priest from California who just finished his third Camino. He concelebrated the pilgrim Mass, which was well-attended by perhaps 800 people. We saw many pilgrims we recognized from our Camino, including Marianne from Germany and Kath from New Zealand. It was a moving experience.

It was fun to hang around in the cathedral plaza, watch newly arrived pilgrims enter the square with such joy and anticipation, greet others we spent time with along the way, and just generally soak in the vibe. Among those I was most anxious to meet as they arrived were Heide and Reinhardt, the German *pilger* Joe and I befriended in 2016. This was Reinhardt's tenth Camino and Heide's fourth. What amazing people they are.

Two days after arriving in Santiago, Craig and I quit our low-rent lodgings, checked into a nice hotel near the university, walked to the bus station, and went to the airport. Though the rain came down in sheets, it was as if we could hear songbirds and see rainbows. Thirty minutes later Aer Lingus flight 742 from Dublin opened its doors and out walked Carol and Dar. I was very, very happy, and even more grateful.

Two grateful pilgrims with those they love—finally.

A pilgrimage is a *solemn thing of mystic meaning*[1]—a sacred journey to a sacred place for a sacred purpose. It has been three years since Craig and I walked into Santiago. Since the pilgrimage finished, I have taken some time to think about its impact on me—for both the short and long term. I am very grateful for its many blessings and insights. My pilgrimage of gratitude has sharpened my focus on the many ways God has blessed me. My heart has been turned in such a way that my own desires have slowly, gradually—and hopefully, permanently—receded and made space for what God calls me to do. This used to scare me. Now it doesn't. Now I welcome it. I can finally place the challenges of 2016 into a broader perspective, grateful for the gifts that I now consider them to have been.

Two grateful pilgrims at the end of the road.

How shall we be grateful for God's love, and why? With the psalmist's guidance I conclude this memoir with gratitude for each person who took the time to read it:

1. Johnson and Troiano, *Roads from Bethlehem*, 29–30.

Praise the LORD, for he is good;
for his mercy endures forever;
Praise the God of gods;
for his mercy endures forever;
Praise the Lord of lords;
for his mercy endures forever;
Who alone has done great wonders,
for his mercy endures forever;
Who skillfully made the heavens,
for his mercy endures forever;
Who spread the earth upon the waters,
for his mercy endures forever;
Who made the great lights,
for his mercy endures forever;
The sun to rule the day,
for his mercy endures forever;
The moon and stars to rule the night,
for his mercy endures forever;
Who struck down the firstborn of Egypt,
for his mercy endures forever;
And led Israel from their midst,
for his mercy endures forever;
With mighty hand and outstretched arm,
for his mercy endures forever;
Who split in two the Red Sea,
for his mercy endures forever;
And led Israel through its midst,
for his mercy endures forever;
But swept Pharaoh and his army into the Red Sea,
for his mercy endures forever;
Who led the people through the desert,
for his mercy endures forever;
Who struck down great kings
for his mercy endures forever;
Slew powerful kings,
for his mercy endures forever;
Sihon, king of the Amorites,
for his mercy endures forever;
Og, king of Bashan,
for his mercy endures forever;
And made their lands a heritage,
for his mercy endures forever;

A heritage for Israel, his servant,
for his mercy endures forever.
The Lord remembered us in our low estate,
for his mercy endures forever;
Freed us from our foes,
for his mercy endures forever;
And gives bread to all flesh,
for his mercy endures forever.
Praise the God of heaven,
for his mercy endures forever. (Ps 136)

Richard Ray
Ash Wednesday, 2022
Holland, Michigan

Interested in learning more about the backstory to *Walking Gratefully*? Consider reading *The Shape of My Heart*, Richard Ray's memoir of grace and healing during his first pilgrimage on the Camino de Santiago. Here's an excerpt:

Preparing to Begin

T HERE's more than one kind of suffering.

I thought I'd toughened my feet up from the endless walking. I'd get home from an all-day hike of twenty miles or so, strip my socks off and stare at the natural disaster that was my feet. Flat where they should be gracefully arched. Pasty white, with crooked toes and blackened toenails. Callused in all the necessary places, or so I thought. Sometimes the skin on top of my feet was sprinkled with a million small, red bumps. Prickly heat. I thought I'd prepared my feet. Still, the long slog up the treadmill of stones that was the approach to the Matagrande Plain with its tantalizing view of Burgos on the far horizon reached through the soles of my Hoka trail runners and gave me my first blister. I felt the slightest zing of discomfort on the side of my left big toe as I powered up the endless incline, eager to get to the city and our first day's rest on the Camino. When I arrived at the *albergue* in Cardeñuela de Riopico and removed my socks, there it was. A fat, throbbing bulge that made my already ugly toe into something even more Gaudíesque. A good reminder of the dust from which I am made—and to which I will return.

The rocky ascent to the Matagrande Plain

There are, in fact, three kinds of suffering. The first kind is normally temporary—though its effects can last a long time in the form of misguided habits. It's largely caused by the idea that there is some pleasure we wished we had right now, but don't. It's an important form of suffering. We can master it—obtain our freedom from it, really—only over a long time of discipline, self-denial, and the development of right habits. Failure to deal effectively with this kind of suffering eventually leads to the third form of suffering, of which I'll have more to say soon.

But before there can be a third thing there must be a second thing. This is the kind of suffering that Job talks about when he asks:

> Is not life on earth a drudgery,
> its days like those of a hireling?
> Like a slave who longs for the shade,
> a hireling who waits for wages,
> So I have been assigned months of futility,
> and troubled nights have been counted off for me. (Job 7:1–3)

Job lost his family, his health, his worldly goods, and pretty much everything else during his terrible trials. Everyone experiences this kind of suffering in one form or another. To be human means to endure loss, hardship, bereavement, death, and the isolating pain of loneliness. It's just the way life is. Jesus himself—Jesus the human being—was sorely tempted by all the things that tempt me. And he knew suffering, and not just suffering on the cross. He cried real tears when his friend Lazarus died—even in the sure knowledge that God would raise him up again, and soon. St. Augustine reminds us:

> *We progress by means of trial.*
> *No one knows himself except through trial.*[1]

Of course, how we respond to this kind of suffering matters. And what also matters is how we respond when we encounter Job's lament in others, including others who are hard to like, much less love. If we get this wrong we really do damage to ourselves and to others around us. To overcome this kind of suffering requires a mature prayer life, and a mature prayer life is one where prayer is a habit. A life where we pray without ceasing. It is this kind of prayer life that casts our gaze toward Him whose mercy endures forever. Without this habit of prayer we are unlikely to look beyond the suffering of the moment to the gratitude that endures. And without gratitude for the blessings that come from the One in whose image and likeness we have been made, well, life really is just the sackcloth and ash that Job describes.

And there is a third kind of suffering to which I alluded earlier. This is the form of suffering that I want to focus on in this account of my pilgrimage on the Camino de Santiago. This is the kind of suffering that Dante Alighieri wrote about in *The Divine Comedy*.[2] The story opens with Dante describing the journey of his life. He finds himself in a dark forest where "the straightforward pathway had been lost." And he suddenly realizes this about his life: he does not know where he is, how he got there, or how he lost his way. Dante is basically saying, "I'm going in the wrong direction." And he is saying one additional thing. A critical thing. Maybe the most important thing. He admits that he was the one who lost the path. He does not claim that anyone else forced him from the true way. He doesn't point to his left or

---

1. Augustine, "Office of Readings."
2. Alighieri, *Divine Comedy*, 1.

his right and shout, "He made me do it!" or "I was tricked. It's not my fault!" Good old Dante. He does a very hard thing. He tells the truth.

I was fired from my job in 2016. I cannot say for sure what led to my dismissal. College politics is a lot like the state of nature Thomas Hobbes described in his seventeenth-century *Leviathan*: "nasty and brutish."[3] I can say without question that I was suffering as a result, and badly. I became angry and, despite my best efforts to the contrary, a bit depressed. Understandably, I viewed my dismissal as an injustice that wounded both my family and me. This anger put me on the wrong path. I grew frightened of where it might lead. I realized that if I didn't renounce this anger-filled way of life and the corrosive thoughts in which it was comfortably, deliciously, satisfyingly clothed I would spend my senior years—my "golden years"—as a bitter old man, a shriveled Golem-like version of myself.

Anger fills us with a sense of disordered righteousness. Anger feels wonderful, like a drug. We rage, we thunder with anger, and when we do we imagine ourselves to be armored in truth and justice. But it's all just foolish pride. Anger distorts our view of who we really are—and who others really are—just like a fun-house mirror. Yes, the path I was on—like the one Dante walked—had a sign that read, *"Abandon all hope, ye who enter here."*

It slowly dawned on me that anger and the suffering it was causing did not have to be the final word. Suffering did not have to be the ultimate condition that defined my life. For just as surely as I could see Dante's warning flashing in big, neon colors, through the grace of a God who is too big for me to understand, I could also see another sign, this one from the prophet Jeremiah:

> *Stand by the earliest roads,*
> *ask the pathways of old,*
> *"Which is the way to good?" and walk it;*
> *thus you will find rest for yourselves. (Jer 6:16)*

I was at Mass one Sunday a few weeks after my job ended when my longtime friend, Joe, approached me and said, "I'm thinking of making a pilgrimage on the Camino de Santiago. Want to come?" The Camino had been a bucket list thing for me for a number of years. A mutual friend of ours, Fr. Steve Dudek, made the pilgrimage in 2006. Listening to his stories animated my thinking ever since. Did I want to go? Of course I did, but I recognized that I owed Carol a conversation, given the expense in dollars

---

3. Hobbes, *Leviathan*, 289.

and time apart. Joe and I agreed that we would have coffee in two weeks to see where things stood.

My professional downfall was not hard only on me. Carol suffered terribly, and had a very difficult time going to work at the same college at which I worked. Even the stroll across campus to her office engendered powerful emotions. The fact that she supported me in such an unqualified way when I asked for her blessing on my pilgrimage is a gift for which I will always be grateful. Still, being absent from her for six weeks working out my anger while she languished at home is something that felt—and still feels—very selfish. Every step I took on my pilgrimage was filled with gratitude for her love.

The Camino de Santiago—literally "the Way of St. James"—is one of Christendom's oldest and most important pilgrimage journeys. Medieval pilgrims began their pilgrimage from wherever they lived and walked to the Cathedral of Santiago de Compostela in northwest Spain, where tradition claims the body of St. James the Apostle rests. While most modern pilgrims begin the journey in Sarria and only walk the last one hundred kilometers, Joe and I would meet pilgrims who began their walks in Germany, Austria, Hungary, the Netherlands, England, Ireland, and many other places.

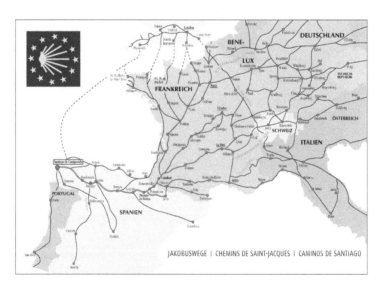

JAKOBUSWEGE | CHEMINS DE SAINT-JACQUES | CAMINOS DE SANTIAGO

Joe and I would walk the "French Way," though there are many routes leading to Santiago de Compostela. (Manfred Zentgraf/Wikimedia Commons/CC BY 3.0)

Would we be walking to the actual burial site of St. James? I hadn't the faintest idea.[4] Martin Luther—no fan of pilgrimages—is said to have quipped, "There were twelve apostles, and eighteen of them are buried in Spain."[5] What I do know—and this is my testimony—is that I hoped our five-hundred-mile walk would be a kind of long-form retreat that would teach me how to pray without ceasing, lead me to forgive my enemies, and help me to seek God's forgiveness for my own brokenness. I hoped to become a new creation on the Camino. I hoped to rediscover the True Way, and thus put behind me the third form of suffering.

4. Andrew Boorde, a sixteenth-century physician-pilgrim was told by a resident priest to whom he confessed his sins that Charlemagne had removed all the relics of St. James to Toulouse many centuries before. Starkie, *Road to Santiago*, 54. This did not stop Pope Leo XIII from visiting Santiago de Compostela and officially certifying the remains. The pope described it in the bull *Omnipotens Deus*, published on November 1, 1884.

5. Hammond, *Luther.*

Bibliography

Alighieri, Dante. *Divine Comedy*, Longfellow's Translation, Complete. S.I.: Pub One Info, n.d.

"Amazing Facts about the Cuckoo." *One Kind Planet*. https://onekindplanet.org/animal/cuckoo/.

Anonymous. "The Introverted Pilgrim." https://www.caminodesantiago.me/community/threads/the-introverted-pilgrim.65949/.

APS News. "Zero Gravity: The Lighter Side of Science: Scientists Prove Kansas Flatter than a Pancake." 12.10 (2003). https://www.aps.org/publications/apsnews/200310/pancake-kansas.cfm.

Aquinas, Thomas. *The Aquinas Prayer Book: The Prayers and Hymns of St. Thomas Aquinas*. Translated by Johann Moser and Robert Anderson. Bedford, NH: Sophia Institute, 2000.

Augustine, Saint. *Confessions*. Translated by John K. Ryan. New York: Doubleday, 1960.

———. "Homily 7 on the First Epistle of John." https://www.newadvent.org/fathers/170207.htm.

———. "Office of Readings." http://www.liturgies.net/Liturgies/Catholic/loh/ lent/week1sundayor.htm

Ausprey, Ian J., and Mark E. Hauber. "Host and Brood Parasite Coevolutionary Interactions Covary with Comparative Patterns of the Avian Visual System." *Biology Letters* 17 (2021). https://royalsocietypublishing.org/doi/pdf/10.1098/rsbl.2021.0309.

BBC World Update. "What Does Hell Smell Like?" Audio, 4:04. https://www.bbc.co.uk/programmes/p03roljl.

Bremer, Thomas S. "A Touristic Spirit in Places of Religion." In *Faith in America: Changes, Challenges, New Directions, Volume 2: Religious Issues Today*, edited by Charles H. Lippy, 2:37-57. 3 vols. Westport, CT: Greenwood, 2006.

Briggs, Katharine Mary. *An Encyclopedia of Fairies: Hobgoblins, Brownies, Bogies, and Other Supernatural Creatures*. New York: Pantheon, 1976.

Bunyan, John. *Pilgrim's Progress in Modern English*. Shallotte, NC: Sovereign Grace, 2008.

"Cædmon's Hymn." Translation by Michael R. Burch. http://www.thehypertexts.com/Best%20Thanksgiving%20Poems%20and%20Poems%20of%20Gratitude.htm.

Cavendish, Richard. "Death of Cesare Borgia." *History Today* 57.3 (2007). https://www.historytoday.com/archive/months-past/death-cesare-borgia.

Clare, John. *Selected Poems*. Edited by Geoffrey Summerfield. London: Penguin, 2000.

Davies, William. *Bernhard Von Breydenbach and His Journey to the Holy Land, 1483–84: A Bibliography.* London: Leighton, 1911.

Dickens, Charles. *Nicholas Nickleby.* Illustrated by Hablot K. Browne. London: Penguin, 1999.

Dreckman, Jessi. "GHS Grad Experiences Life-Changing Pilgrimage." *Ozark Country Times,* June 20, 2019. http://www.ozarkcountytimes.com/news-local-news/ghs-grad-experiences-life-changing-pilgrimage.

Epictetus. *The Handbook (The Encheiridion).* Translated by Nicholas B. White. Indianapolis: Hackett, 1983.

Fakes, Dennis. *G.R.A.C.E.: The Essence of Spirituality.* Lincoln, NE: Writers Showcase, 2002.

Fatherhorton. "St. Teresa of Ávila and the Weather." *Fauxtations,* January 25, 2015. https://fauxtations.wordpress.com/2015/01/25/st-teresa-of-avila-and-the-weather/.

Fletcher, Richard A. *The Quest for El Cid.* Oxford: Oxford University Press, 1989.

Frauca, Jesús Arraiza. "De Pamplona a Puente La Reina." *Peregrino: revista del Camino de Santiago* 46 (1995) 12–13.

Galloway, Lindsey. "The UK's Longest Named Village." *BBC,* March 20, 2012. https://www.bbc.com/travel/article/20120320-worldwide-weird-the-uks-longest-named-village.

Gitlitz, David M., and Linda Kay Davidson. *The Pilgrimage Road to Santiago: The Complete Cultural Handbook.* New York: St. Martin's, 2000.

Hall, Linda B. *Mary, Mother and Warrior: The Virgin in Spain and the Americas.* Austin: University of Texas Press, 2009.

Hammond, Peter. "Film Review: Luther." ReformationSA.org. http://www.reformationsa.org/index.php/component/content/article/61-film-reviews/167-film-review-luther.

Harms, Matthew, et al. *Camino de Santiago, Camino Frances: St Jean - Santiago - Finisterre.* Village to Village Guide. Harrisonburg, VA: Village to Village, 2018.

Hill, Edmund, and John E. Rotelle. *Letters 100–155.* Hyde Park, NY: New City, 1990.

"Historical Events on May 15." *On This Day.* https://www.onthisday.com/events/may/15.

Hobbes, Thomas. *Leviathan.* Edited by John Charles Addison Gaskin. Oxford World's Classics. Oxford: Oxford University Press, 1998.

Jason, Zachary. "A Deliberate Walk: Students in a New Philosophy Class Hike Spain's Camino de Santiago." *Boston College News,* July 10, 2015. https://www.bc.edu/bc-web/bcnews/humanities/philosophyandethics/Caminopilgrimage.html.

John Paul II, Pope. "*Message of the Holy Father John Paul II to the Youth of the World on the Occasion of the IV World Youth Day (Santiago De Compostela, August 1989.*" *Vatican. va,* November 27, 1988. https://www.vatican.va/content/john-paul-ii/en/messages/youth/documents/hf_jp-ii_mes_27111988_iv-world-youth-day.html.

———. "*Novo Millennio Ineunte.*" *Vatican.va,* January 6, 2001. https://www.vatican.va/content/john-paul-ii/en/apost_letters/2001/documents/hf_jp-ii_apl_20010106_novo-millennio-ineunte.html.

Johnson, Pegram, III, and Edna M. Troiano. *The Roads from Bethlehem: Christmas Literature from Writers Ancient and Modern.* Louisville: Presbyterian, 1993.

Josephson, Peter, et al., eds. *The Humboldtian Tradition: Origins and Legacies.* Leiden: Brill, 2014.

Keillor, Garrison. "The Art of Love in the Far North." http://www.garrisonkeillor.com/the-art-of-love-in-the-far-north/.

Lewis, C. S. *The Pilgrim's Regress.* Grand Rapids: Eerdmans, 2014.

———. *The Weight of Glory.* London: HarperCollins, 2001.

Logsdon, Gene. *Holy Shit: Managing Manure to Save Mankind.* White River Junction, VT: Chelsea Green, 2010.

Longfellow, Henry W. "Snow-flakes." *Poetry Foundation.* https://www.poetryfoundation. org/poems/44649/snow-flakes.

Lovasik, Lawrence G. *The Basic Book of Catholic Prayer: How to Pray and Why.* Manchester, NH: Sophia, 1999.

Marlowe, Christopher. "The Passionate Shepherd to His Love." In *The Complete Poems and Translations,* edited by Stephen Orgel, 207. New York: Penguin, 2007.

Merton, Thomas. *The Seven Storey Mountain.* New York: HarperCollins, 1998.

"Mesa." *National Geographic.* https://education.nationalgeographic.org/resource/mesa.

Munro, Eleanor. *On Glory Roads: A Pilgrims' Book about Pilgrimage.* New York: Thames and Hudson, 1987.

Oficina de Acogida al Perigrino, Catedral de Santiago. *Informe Estadístico.* http:// oficinadelperegrino.com/wp-content/uploads/2016/02/peregrinaciones2019.pdf.

Ordish, T. Fairman. "St. Crispin's Day." *The Antiquary* (1882) 137–44.

Orlin, Lena Cowen. "A Case for Anecdotalism in Women's History: The Witness Who Spoke When the Cock Crowed." *English Literary Renaissance* 31.1 (2001) 52–77.

Palmer, Craig T., et al. "In Defense of Differentiating Pilgrimage from Tourism." *International Journal of Tourism Anthropology* 2.1 (2012) 71–85.

Parkes, Bessie Rayner. *Poems.* London: John Chapman, 1855.

Pederson, E. O. "Sheep and the Camino." https://americanpilgrims.org/wp-content/ uploads/2019/04/essays_camino_sheep.pdf.

Preston, Paul. *A People Betrayed: A History of Corruption, Political Incompetence and Social Division in Modern Spain.* New York: Liveright, 2020.

Ray, Richard. *The Shape of My Heart: A Pilgrimage Remembrance.* Eugene, OR: Resource, 2022.

"Sheep Replace Cars as They Cross Madrid En Route to Winter Pastures." Reuters, October 24, 2021. (https://www.reuters.com/lifestyle/oddly-enough/sheep-replace-cars-they-cross-madrid-en-route-winter-pastures-2021-10-24/) 2021.

Smith, James K. A. *You Are What You Love: The Spiritual Power of Habit.* Grand Rapids: Brazos, 2016.

Snell, R. J. "Quiet Hope: A New Year's Resolution." *Public Discourse,* December 31, 2019. https://www.thepublicdiscourse.com/2019/12/59322/.

Starkie, Walter. *The Road to Santiago: Pilgrims of St. James.* London: Murray, 1957.

Stevenson, Robert Louis. "In the Highlands." *Victorian Poetry* 34.2 (Summer 1996) 212.

Tabori, Lena, and Natasha Tabori Fried. *A Little Book of Love Poems and Letters.* Kansas City, MO: Andrews McMeel, 2001.

Taylor, Allen. *American Colonies: The Settling of North America.* New York: Penguin, 2002.

Turner, Victor. *Dramas, Fields, and Metaphors: Symbolic Action in Human Society.* Reading, UK: Ithaca, 1974.

United Nations Educational, Scientific, and Cultural Organization. "Archaeological Site of Atapuerca." https://whc.unesco.org/en/list/989/.

———. "Burgos Cathedral." https://whc.unesco.org/en/list/316/.

Upile, Tahwinder, et al. "The Acute Effects of Alcohol on Auditory Thresholds." *BMC Ear Nose Throat Disorders* 7.4 (2007). https://doi.org/10.1186/1472-6815-7-4.

Watts, Linda. "The Stork." In *American Myths, Legends, and Tall Tales: An Encyclopedia of American Folklore,* edited by Christopher R. Fee and Jeffrey B. Webb, 897–900. Santa Barbara, CA: ABC-CLIO, 2016.

Weber, David K. "*Buen Camino*: Blessed Are Those Whose Hearts Are Set on Pilgrimage." *The Cresset* 83.1 (2019) 47–49.

Wharton, Edith, and Irene Goldman-Price. *Selected Poems of Edith Wharton*. New York: Scribner, 2019.

Wiesenthal, Simon. *The Sunflower: On the Possibilities and Limits of Forgiveness*. London: Knopf Doubleday, 2008.

Wolff, Leon. *In Flanders Fields: The 1917 Campaign*. London: Penguin, 1979.

Lightning Source UK Ltd.
Milton Keynes UK
UKHW021830030223
416442UK00004B/11